In Times Like These

*Words of Comfort in a Time of Chaos,
Conflict, and Confusion*

Pastor Robby Stewart

ISBN 978-1-63961-991-7 (paperback)
ISBN 978-1-63961-992-4 (digital)

Christian Faith Publishing
832 Park Avenue
Meadville, PA 16335
www.christianfaithpublishing.com

Note: All scriptures will be KJV unless otherwise noted.

Cover Art designed by Jan Allen

Printed in the United States of America

Acknowledgments

First of all, I would like to thank God for his many mercies and the abundance of grace he has given unto me during my years of serving him and allowing me to accomplish this work that you are holding in your hands. May he bless you with all spiritual blessings and encourage you to a strong faith, good graces, and a hope that will make you not ashamed during these most challenging times.

I would like to thank my mom and dad for their part in making this work possible through their prayers and generosity, and may God restore it back into them in manifold ways.

To the congregation of Crestview Baptist Church, I would like to acknowledge all of their love and support unto me, their pastor, in one of the most challenging times in our country. Their patience and understanding throughout this pandemic with all of its challenges help me to see the kind of patience that our Lord Jesus and James spoke of in the scriptures. May God continue to bless the people of Crestview until the day Christ comes again.

As in my previous work, *For Such a Time as This*, I would like to thank Kathy Crouch for all of her time and effort in editing these reflections and meditations. Her devotional life and honest critique are well appreciated, and she is just as much a part of this book as I am. Also, a special shout out to Sara Adkins who in a time of crises developed our Facebook group page in order for us to stream our services and open the door for these daily devotions to come about.

I would like to thank my family for their longtime faithful love and support throughout all of these years of ministry. My wife, Vickie, has always been a source of strength and encouragement to me, and her wisdom and understanding have always been timely. To our two children, Kennedi and Jeremiah, I am so grateful for their support and encouragement to me and for the life that they both have lived that glorifies God and makes me and their mother so very proud. To Jared, my son-in-law, who is a very good husband to Kennedi and knows how to make me laugh with his wit and wisdom.

Finally, I would not have been able to accomplish a task such as this without mentioning some mentors and friends whom God placed in my life down through the years. Bruce Goodwin, a mentor and dear friend gone on to be with the Lord who taught me how to study. Sam Jarrell, also with the Lord, a mentor and one who taught me about grace. C. J. Bordeux, who was a dear friend and an encouragement to me on a daily basis in whom God called home in his time but way too early for us who knew and loved him. To two dear friends, Pastor Mike Childers and Pastor Billy Dennis, for their deep spiritual insight and their lightheartedness. Last but not least, Pastor Jerry Goins, who asked me to play the Prodigal Son on Sunday morning, June 22, 1997. I was a true prodigal when I walked into the church, but I left the church that same day as a born-again Christian.

There are many others whom I could mention, but time and space would not allow it. God knows who they are, and may he reward them greatly in the age to come.

Pastor Robby

Preface

As our country was overwhelmed by the COVID-19 pandemic, no one thought that it would have had the long-lasting effects that it did. What was believed in the beginning to be one of the most unique years in modern history and a brief setback in our everyday way of life lasted through the summer of 2020 and gained momentum once again in the fall. Once 2021 came around, the reality set in that this may not just be a once-in-a-lifetime event in our generation but something we may have to learn to live with and change the way we live permanently. For the first time ever, Thanksgiving and Christmas were spent alone or, at best, with just a small group of family members. Schools were meeting online, and dropout rates were at an all-time high. Because of the closing of many public places, boredom set in, which led to an increase in drug addiction, mental health commitments, abuse, and suicide. With many churches not meeting, our country saw church attendance and the desire for the ways of God steadily decline into an all-time low. As a pastor, my heart ached during this period of time, and for the first time, I realized the challenge that lay before me to shepherd the flock that God had given me to watch over.

In Times Like These was one of the tools that God used to help me and the people of Crestview Baptist Church navigate our way through. What began as a series of daily Facebook posts in March of 2020 and collected in the first book published in 2021 titled *For Such a Time as This*, the meditations and reflections in this book are the continuation of those daily posts that helped us stay *focused, connected, and encouraged* in difficult times. Not only were we still dealing with the pandemic but also the riots that occurred throughout our nation as a result of the George Floyd death in Minnesota;

the chaos in Portland, Oregon; and the temporary takeover of the city of Seattle, Washington. Finally, to end out the year, there was the controversy of the presidential election, ultimately culminating in the storming of the Capitol Building on January 6, 2021. These were definitely challenging times, and what our country needed more than anything was a church that was ready and equipped for the challenge.

It is during these times of crises that we desire to hear the voice of God more than ever. I believe that one of the ways he spoke was through these series of devotions. *In Times Like These* is not just timely for our national crises but for our own personal crises as well. I tried to remain as faithful to the Word of God as I possibly could be so that, in generations to come, these words will still be relevant, timely, and, most of all, encouraging to all the hands God places this work in.

May God bless this work and all who read it. Unto him be all the glory and honor. Amen!

Table of Contents

In Times Like These

(A prayer inspired by Luke 21:5–36 KJV)

Heavenly Father, I thank you, Lord, that in times like these, we have a place of refuge and quietness. I praise you, Lord, that you are a source of peace and calm in troubling times. I thank you that you are a pillar of strength in our weakness.

I am grateful that when I am not sure, there is a surer word of prophecy that is a light in dark times. I acknowledge your ordered providence in a seemingly chaotic world. I know that all things are working together for good to them that love you and are called according to your purpose.

I pray to have faith in not what I see but in what I know and who I know in the person of your Son Jesus Christ. I ask that in times like these, you will help me be patient, knowing that in my patience I possess my soul. I pray to be focused on Christ by looking up and unto him, knowing our redemption is drawing nigh. And, Lord, I pray to watch and pray always that I will be worthy to escape all these things that are coming to pass and to stand before the Son of Man. I desire not to just say my prayers but to breathe them. May prayer be air to my spiritual health and your word be nourishment to my soul. Last

of all, Lord, in times like these, help me be a good
witness of your saving grace and be salt and light
in a dark world.

In Jesus's name, I pray. Amen!

A Clear Vision and a Sure Word
(Matthew 17:1–8 and 1 Peter 1:16–21)

After watching the presidential debate this week, I am left with just
this one thought—I feel like I have blurry vision. After about an hour
and a half of mudslinging, I am still not sure where we are heading.

I love what Ravi Zacharias said about mudslinging. He said,
"When you sling mud, you do two things. You get your hands dirty,
and you lose a lot of ground." Obviously, he was being satirical, but
within his satire, there is a truth. Who won the debate? I am not
really sure, but the one thing I know for sure is that if we continue at
this pace, America loses.

It really shows us the bankruptcy of partisan politics. Name-
calling and character assassination has replaced policy and procedure.
All we can really do is hope that through all the explosiveness, a single
successful vision of the future will come forth for our country. But as
Christians, we know that the vision of the future goes far beyond our
heritage. There is a greater vision; there is a better country. There is a
surer word of prophecy that gives us a clear vision of where history is
going. It's going right where God wants it to. It finds its completion
in the reign of Jesus Christ, who is King of kings and Lord of lords,
whose kingdom will never be destroyed.

Peter, James, and John got a glimpse of this kingdom on the
Mount of Transfiguration. The flesh of the eternal Christ was rolled
back, and they saw him in the brightness of his glory. They wanted
to make Moses and Elijah a tabernacle, a place of worship along with
Jesus, but a cloud overshadowed them. And the voice of God the
Father spoke, "This is my beloved son in whom I am well pleased,
listen to him." After this, Jesus touched them and told them to arise,
and the Scripture records, "They saw no man save Jesus only."

Peter records this event in 2 Peter 1:16–21. He explains that the transfiguration experience was amazing. But as with all experiences, they come and go. He talks about something that is surer than experience. He talks about the surety of God's Word.

So what do we learn from these two accounts?

First, visions are good, but if we do not adhere to those visions, then they are fleeting. Experiences fail because we tend to want new ones. We have two visions laid out before us in this election, but every vision must be grounded in a constant. In this case, the constant is in the Word of God.

Second, the Bible does offer us a vision for our nation and how it can be sustained: building on the principles of law and order revealed through the Ten Commandments and the ethics of Christ's Sermon on the Mount. But we see how we are trending away from that which is sure to that which is constantly shifting. Two places in the Old Testament tell us the importance of a single and sustainable vision. The Hebrew word for "vision" can be translated as "Word of the Lord" (Proverbs 29:18 and Hosea 4:6). For without it, the people perish.

Lastly, for the Christian, the future looks very bright. When Christ was transfigured, his countenance was so bright that they couldn't look upon him. One day when he comes again, we will be changed into his likeness, and we will be able to behold the brightness of his glory in the fullness of his kingdom.

If we think the American ideal and the vision of our framers was great in its outworking, how much more the vision laid out before us in the Bible of the coming kingdom of Christ. It is so bright that the sun, moon, and stars will pale in comparison. And there will be no need of them. And even our leaders, those faithful men and women who are trying to build our nation on that same biblical vision, too will one day pale in comparison to Jesus Christ, as every knee will bow and every tongue will confess that Jesus Christ is Lord!

What a vision! But more than that, what a surety!

A Conversion Poem

(Mark 5:1–20)

When I consider the meaning of life,
I know that my purpose lies in something greater
than me.
Are we here by accident as they would have us to
believe?
Or is there someone that is greater than me?
The world outside seems so ordered and
consistent,
but within me, there is chaos, something volatile
to my existence.
Is there no peace that can be found within,
something that I can grasp that keeps me from
being tossed?
I feel that there are a thousand different voices
and thoughts
that pull me apart so that I feel torn,
pulled in every direction, taking me away from
all that is me.
But lo, I look and see, coming from afar,
a beauty that no one beholds because of his scars.
I see him withered, battered, and bruised,
and yet I wonder how could such one endures
such suffering.
I am compelled to run to him though the voices
say, "Flee."
I go to him in desperation,

knowing that he, though himself beaten and torn, can help me.
I fall down before him, and he speaks,
but it is as though he is speaking to someone besides me.
I hear these voices as they respond to his command;
with such authority, his voice in no way can they withstand.
Come out of him is what's he says,
and all of sudden, I feel peace, calm, and no dread.
Having come to myself and notice my nakedness and shame,
I feel the urgency to clothe myself
and cover the scars of my anguish and pain.
You see, I now know that I am healed by the peace that I have.
I still hear a voice, not voices, and that voice brings me to calm.
This man's name is Jesus, and he made the whole world that is beautiful, ordered, and sustained,
but what I observed outside of me now has been created within.
When I consider the meaning of life,
I know that my purpose lies in something greater in me.
But that something is someone who created me for a purpose,
that has made me greater than I ever imagine I could be.

A Devotional Prayer
(Luke 18:1)

Good morning! This is a devotional prayer that the Lord moved upon me to write this morning. You may be at a loss for words this morning as you go to prayer. I pray that this will help you enter into God's presence.

> Heavenly Father, I come before you this morning with a tender heart, giving thanks for another day. I have come to offer myself to you as a living sacrifice, holy and acceptable unto you by the blood of Jesus Christ. It is in him that I live, move, and have my being. And I know that without him, I am nothing and can do nothing. Yet I can do all things through Christ which strengthens me. For nothing is impossible with you, Lord.
>
> I come before you this morning, offering up my prayer and supplication with thanksgiving making known unto my request. There are many things I want, but I come to you asking to meet my need. For I know that through Christ, all my needs shall be supplied according to his riches in glory.
>
> I need grace for my journey, mercy that never fails, forgiveness for my sins, a heart that is pure, a mind that is like Christ, hope that makes me not ashamed, and the fullness of the Holy Spirit. I desire eyes to see what you see, ears to hear the Spirit, compassion for those who are lost, and a love for my enemies. Help me hate the things you hate, love the things you love, be grieved by what grieves you, and rejoice in what you rejoice in. And when my heart begins to fail today, be my shield, my glory, and the lifter of my head. These are the things I need. What I want is your will to be done on earth and in me, as it is done in heaven. I want to have a tender heart and a teachable spirit. And I want for others as I would want for myself. I know that I have not asked anything too hard for you and all

these things are what you want for me. Last of all, not only do I need to love you with all my heart, soul, mind, and strength and love my neighbor as myself but I want too as well.

All these things I ask with the expectation to be answered for your name's sake and glory. I also ask them in the light of your coming, praying fervently, "Even so come, Lord Jesus!"

May your grace be with us all! In Jesus's name, I pray! Amen!

A Place for the Weary
(John 4:6)

Jesus, our Lord, is weary! He has been on a long journey to meet just one downcast woman in whom he sees as precious. She has been rejected by men, society, and religious people. Yet Christ comes to her. Not in strength and power but weary and humble. He is sitting by Jacob's well, and she is coming to draw from it. What an opportunity for good when these two worlds collide.

What lessons can we learn from this most beautiful of all sacred text?

First, we learn just how human Jesus was. He was tired, thirsty, and weary. It's hard to imagine that God in the flesh could feel this way, yet we see just how much he identifies with our physical and spiritual challenges.

Second, we learn that he went all this way to speak to one person, and not a person of nobility, fame, or even respect but one who was despised and rejected by men. Jesus could identify with her pain because as Isaiah said, he too would be despised and rejected by men. But what we learn from Jesus is that he took a far journey from heaven to earth to die for all men and women, even if you or I were the only one.

Finally, we learn from Jesus that there is a place we can go to when we are weary. He went to a well to meet this woman. You and I go to the well to meet with him! He not only meets us at the well, he is the well of living water that springs up to everlasting life. When we are tired and thirsty, we can go to him and find rest near to the heart of God, for Jesus is the heart of God.

There is an old hymn we sing that says, "There is a place of quiet rest, near to the heart of God."

I know that we are all weary and heavy-laden, but there is a place of refreshment that we are invited to at any and every moment of our journey. But what makes this place so special is that it is not the place but the person who is waiting there for us. The person of Jesus Christ.

Jesus said, "If any man thirsts, let him come unto me and drink" (John 7:37). Meet with Christ today and let him fill your cup so that it may run over and bring refreshment to your dry and thirsty soul.

A Place to Hide
(Revelation 6:15–17 and Colossians 3:1–4)

During the great day of God's wrath, it will be a time of accountability. When the realization of the judgment comes, it is then that mankind will realize they are accountable for their sins. According to John in Revelation, they will try to hide under the mountains in caves, praying that the rocks will conceal them from the flaming eyes and fiery wrath of Christ.

The Bible tell us in many places that it is impossible to hide from God. Man, like Adam, has tried to hide from God when it came time to own up to his disobedience but has failed in his attempts. The psalmist in Psalms 139:7 says, "Whither shall I go from thy spirit? Or whither shall I flee from your presence?" God is an all-knowing God and an ever-present God, and there is no one or nothing that is hidden from him.

Judgment is inevitable because Hebrews 9:27 says, "It is appointed unto man once to die and then the judgement." There is simply no way around our appointment with God, and as we stand before him, there will be nothing covered or hidden from him. There appears to be nowhere to hide. Or is there?

There is one place that God has made available to hide in his time of wrath and judgment. That place is found in Jesus! Paul said in Colossians 3:3 that we are "hid in Christ." God's judgment for sin came upon Jesus at the cross, and all who come to the cross are under the covering of his blood by which "we have redemption, even the forgiveness of sins" (Colossians 1:14). Because of Jesus, we pass from judgment unto justification as God declares us righteous. It is a divine declaration and one that cannot not be overruled by a higher court, for there is no greater judge than the Lord our God!

Just as Noah and his family escaped the flood of God's judgment by entering into the ark, we too—by entering into our ark, Jesus Christ—will pass through judgment unto eternal life. God set the rainbow in the sky as a covenant reminder to Noah that he would not flood the earth again. We too have the covenant reminder of the cross and the seal of the Holy Spirit assuring us that "whosoever believes upon Christ, will not perish, but have everlasting life" (John 3:16).

A Prayer for Grace
(Hebrews 4:16)

Heavenly Father and God of all grace, I come before you through Jesus Christ, in whom John said was full of grace and truth. I approach your throne of grace today boldly, confidently, and expectantly, knowing that you will provide the mercy and the grace I need in my time of trouble.

I have sinned against you this day, but I am reminded that where sin abounds, grace much more abounds. I know that I sinned because I am a sinner saved by your grace and cannot offer any good thing unto you to deserve or merit your favor.

Even on my best day, I fall short of your glory, yet I am saved by grace. I have weaknesses, sicknesses, and afflictions. But I am reminded that I also have your grace, which is sufficient for me, and that I may glory in these things and not complain.

I also pray that grace will teach me to deny ungodliness and worldly lust and live soberly, righteously, and godly in this present world.

I know that I can do nothing for you today unless you give me grace to perform it. So work in and through me your goodwill and pleasure that I may be a portrait of your grace today and be conformed to the image of Christ.

In closing, I pray that the grace of our Lord Jesus Christ will be with us all, even unto the end of age, world without end. Amen!

A Prayer for Passion
(1 Timothy 2:3–4)

The death of Jesus on the cross is known as the Passion of Christ. On the cross, we see God's passion and compassion for mankind. His will was that all men would be saved and come to the knowledge of the truth. The Spirit of Christ is within his church. Should this not be our same desire, His passion our passion? May he stir up within us a burden for lost souls. The first step is prayer.

> Father, in the name of your Son Jesus Christ, I come before you today, thanking you for your passion for me and your compassion for my lost soul. Thank you for forgiving me and saving me from my sins and eternity in hell. I thank you that in Christ, I have hope in knowing there is no condemnation to them who believe. I am what I am by your grace that you bestow upon me daily.
>
> But, Lord, I confess that I am not as burdened for others as myself. I confess that I have no passion or compassion for lost souls, especially those in my family, my coworkers, and neighbors.
>
> Having confessed my sin of indifference toward others, I pray that you would stir up the gift of God that is within me to share the good news of the gospel of which I heard and believed. Help me look upon others as you do. Help me see their needs and not be critical of their short-

comings. Help me, as Christ, be willing to extend a hand to those who are unclean like the leper so that they may receive their cleansing by receiving Jesus Christ as their savior.

The time is short! The sheep of America are scattered. The harvest is plenteous, but the laborers are few. Lord, I pray that you would send laborers into the harvest. And let me say as Isaiah, "Here I am, Lord. Send me!"

Lord, give us a harvest of souls. As we go forth weeping bearing precious seed, let us come back rejoicing, bringing our sheaves with us. As you send us forth to make disciples, may we remember that you are with us always, even unto the end of the world!

May the grace of our Lord Jesus Christ and the love of God and the communion of the Holy Spirit be with us all. Amen!

Meditate on these other scriptures to help form your own prayer life and prepare you for soul winning: Matthew 9:36–38, Isaiah 6:1–8, and Psalms 126:6.

A Rose in the Desert
(Isaiah 35:1)

Isaiah said that a rose would bloom in a desert. This has to be the most beautiful scene that can be observed on earth. Whether it be a red, yellow, pink, or white rose against the backdrop of a dry and barren place, it presents a welcome sight for sore eyes. It is not only beautiful but it is fragrant. It lets you and I know that there is beauty among the mundane and life among death.

This is the picture of Jesus Christ! He came into the world as Paul said when the "fullness of time had come." It was the right time because God's people were dry spiritually, barren in prosperity, and under the iron fist of oppressive Rome. Israel was nothing like its glory days in David's and Solomon's times. Yet it was the right time for God to be made flesh and begin his work of salvation among men.

We all want things to be the way they used to be. And I sense the frustration, impatience, bitterness, and uncertainty that is starting to fill our hearts and minds. Things just do not feel right, and we almost feel out of place. As Christians, it shouldn't feel right, and we should feel out of place because this world is not our home. God didn't make us for deserts. He made us for green pastures and still waters. But as our great shepherd leads us in the paths of righteousness, we go through some valleys that are dry, barren, and dark to get to greener pastures and cooler waters.

But along the way, if we look close enough in the backdrop of all that is bad, we can see a rose blooming. Christianity is all about focus. It's all about keeping our eyes and hearts fixed on the person of Christ who is the "rose of Sharon." There are many bad things happening, but God is doing great things too, and it would serve us well to pray and ask him to help us discern those things. It's not about being pessimistic or optimistic, half full or half empty. It's all about a great God doing great things for his people in a time when they need it the most.

So today, in a time when America is spiritually low, barren in spiritual blessings, and oppressed by civil disorder, remember there is a rose that is in bloom. But also remember every rose has its thorns. So too our Lord Jesus Christ, the rose of Sharon, had his crown of thorns. But on the third day, he—in the backdrop of death—arose from the grave and is alive forever more! And because he lives, we will live also.

So seek to find the beauty of God in our world today and in other people. Also, seek to bring forth his beauty in our lives by allowing the Holy Spirit to conform us to his image and likeness. Who knows, maybe you will be a rose to somebody today. One who is beautiful and fragrant in the sight of the Lord!

Read also Galatians 4:4 and Song of Solomon 2:1.

Advent: A Time of Preparation
(Amos 4:1–13)

The second Sunday of Advent is about preparation. Preparation is an important method in life. We prepare our meals. We prepare for our children's college, and athletes prepare for a game. Parties, lessons, and sermons all take preparation. The number 1 thing that most people prepare for today is retirement. All these things take time, money, and sacrifice. But once you arrive at retirement and your child's first day of college or the big wedding is done, you find out it was all worth the time and effort.

Most people plan also for their funerals. They will do what is called a "preneed" so that they can have peace of mind that the expenses are covered and the service is done as they wish. But how many people prepare to meet God? For some, the retirement doesn't come, the wedding plans are canceled, or college has been put on hold. But one thing is for sure, we all will have a meeting with God one day, and we need to be prepared to stand before him.

In our text, God has given Israel one chance after another. He has sent a famine, withheld the rain, smitten with mildew, and sent pestilence to encourage the people to turn back to him. Finally, after much long suffering, he lets them know that mercy, grace, and patience are over and to "prepare to meet God." When we compare the similarities of Israel in Amos's time to the conditions of our day, we notice that God is really doing and saying the same things. In some places, there have been fires and droughts and, in others, hurricanes and flooding. Some cities have endured protests and riots while all of us are still under a pandemic. I don't know how much more God can say or do to get our attention.

With all these things happening in this Advent season, we are reminded that this will be the condition of the world prior to the second coming. Could we be living in the greatest moment that will ever occur in human history, that moment being the return of Jesus? If so, we need to be preparing to meet him.

Preparation involves three things.

First, we must prepare ourselves by making sure that we have accepted Christ as our savior. Every knee will bow, and every tongue will confess that Jesus Christ is Lord. The difference between the Christians and non-Christians is that the Christians willfully bow in this life, surrendering themselves to God, whereas the non-Christian will be forced to do this on the day of judgment.

Second, we prepare ourselves by preparing others. What John the Baptist was in Jesus's first coming, so are we in the second coming. He was a forerunner, and we are as well. We do our very best in sharing our faith and living our lives in holiness. Most importantly, we prepare like he is coming back today, which helps us keep our focus and not be distracted.

Finally, the apostle John assured us that when we stand before God, we can do it confidently (1 John 4:17). This is done by having a perfect love in our hearts for God and one another. A perfect heart is a prepared heart. The church is the bride of Christ. John said in Revelation that she (the church) came down like a bride adorned for her husband (Revelation 21:2). Just as a bride spends days, months, and even years preparing for her wedding day, we too as the church should follow in her example.

Preparing to meet God is the single most important appointment that we will ever have. It is unavoidable. The difference is going to be whether we have prepared or procrastinated.

Read also Luke 3:1–18 for further thoughts on preparation.

Advent Preparation: A Voice Crying in the Wilderness

(Luke 3:1–18)

Every time I read Luke's account of the emergence of John the Baptist, I am amazed at from whom and where God would choose to introduce the long-awaited messiah. It came as Paul described in Galatians 4:4 as "the fullness of time." It was a time of political failure and religious despair. Yet these conditions produced a ripe atmosphere for the Word of God to come, not only in message but also in person!

Notice that John's preaching was not in the temple or synagogue or even on the street corner. No, it was in the wilderness. The message was so simple yet so powerful, as it was delivered not in man's wisdom but in the demonstration and power of the Holy Spirit. His message was one of being prepared for the invasion and intervention of God into the fallen world of humanity to redeem it and reconcile it back to himself. By this, he would create a community that we are a part of today, the community of the church.

There are several things in which we are encouraged to do in order to prepare and be prepared to meet the second invasion and intervention of Christ at his second coming of which we long for and look for in this present Advent season.

First, there is repentance. Repentance simply means to turn from sin and self and look into the face of God. It also means to acknowledge that we have been wrong and that God is right. The work of repentance involves ACT:

- acknowledgment of sin,
- confession of sin, and
- turning away from sin.

By doing this ACT, it prepares us for the coming of Christ.

Second, there is the fruit of repentance. In other words, salvation is an inward work that works its way outward. Fruit of repentance means that the root has been changed, and because of a turning away from sin, we no longer bear the fruit of unrighteousness but of righteousness. The invasion and intervention of Christ in the Christmas story can be seen in the outworking that Paul describes in Romans 6:22–23. Now that we are made free from sin, we have become servants of God and bear the fruit of a holy life. This is done by receiving the gift of God in Jesus Christ.

Finally, John knew that his preparing the world for the coming of Christ was a work that pointed to someone greater than he ever was or would be. We, as the church, have put the spotlight on our buildings, sanctuaries, programs, and eloquent teaching and preaching, forgetting that the gospel was introduced and brought unto us by an eccentric John the Baptist and later on by fishermen, tax collectors, and a host of men and women that came from humble beginnings and changed the world.

Politics and religion have proven themselves to fail and fail miserably. But the Word of God will never fail, and it will always prosper where unto it is sent!

Advent: A Time of Comfort
(Luke 2:25–32 and 1 Thessalonians 4:13–18)

One of the precious commodities in our world today are things that bring us comfort. Whether it is furniture, mattresses, or our favorite comfort foods, we have those things that make us feel good and feel safe in uncomfortable situations.

Simeon had been waiting a long time for the *consolation* of Israel. The word "consolation" means to comfort someone after a time of suffering or loss. Israel had suffered much under Roman oppression and was longing now more than ever for her messiah. Simeon is not only an example of the longing but also of joy when he not only saw Israel's consolation but held it in his arms. The comfort of Israel was not in words or sedatives but in God through his incarnate Son, Jesus Christ.

I have to admit these last few months have been very challenging for me and our church as a whole. As many months have passed, this pandemic is starting to have its toll on many people in many different ways. It is the first time that I have been challenged as a pastor to try to keep us focused, connected, and encouraged. If anything, it has caused me not to long for a postpandemic world but for the return of Christ.

I honestly don't know how anyone could make it day by day without Jesus in times like these. Unlike Simeon who held Jesus in his arms, it is Jesus who holds us in his, and we find strength in him day by day. By going to him in prayer, we find the peace and comfort we need in turbulent times. By reading his Word, we find the words of hope and comfort that guide us through the dark nights of the soul.

During this Advent season, we do have a comfort in the promise of Christ's return. Paul brought comfort to the believers in Thessalonica by reminding them that Jesus will come again and that those who are dead as well as those who are alive will rise up together to meet him in the air and will be with him forever. His admonition to them was to "comfort one another with these words" (1 Thessalonians 4:13–18).

I want to encourage you today with these same words that Paul shared with the Thessalonians. And also with the words of Jesus when he said, "Let not your hearts be troubled!" (John 14:1).

Read also 2 Corinthians 1:3–5.

Advent Living: Commitment
(Psalms 37:5)

The first step in doing anything meaningful is "to commit." Without commitment, many tasks never get done, and what is accomplished is only part of what could have been. Some of the most successful businesspeople—such as artists, musicians, and athletes—are those who commit their lives to their talents, demonstrating unto all that *practice makes perfect*. They spend hours in the office, studio, and on the practice field, only to show off their talent in just a few minutes in the concert hall, museum, or stadium. That is why there are only a few of these great men and women in their fields. Many have the ability but lack in commitment.

To be a good Christian and effective witness for Christ, it takes the same kind of commitment. Our Scripture text says to "commit your ways to the Lord." When we do this, we understand that it takes practice in order to reach spiritual maturity. Salvation comes to us freely, but sanctification is a daily ongoing practice that begins every morning by "presenting our bodies a living sacrifice holy and acceptable unto the Lord" (Romans 12:1).

There are three steps involved in committing ourselves to the Lord on a daily basis.

First, there is *looking to the Lord*. We look to the Lord in prayer and listen to his voice by reading the Bible. This gives us focus by setting our eyes upon him and not the things of the world.

Second, there is *living for the Lord*. Through prayer and listening to God, we have the pattern given unto us on how to live for him daily. The purpose of the Bible is to lead us to and conform us to the image of Jesus. Just as he was the "word made flesh," the word becomes flesh in us as we become doers of the word and not just hearers.

Finally, commitment means *longing for the Lord.* The Bible teaches us that the sure way to be ready for the imminent return of Christ is to live a holy life. By living a life of holiness, we are grieved by what is around us in this fallen, sinful world. This grief eventually leads us to desiring the new heavens and new earth that God has promised. It is then that we long for the return of Jesus to deliver us from this present world.

So commitment means practice. Let us commit our ways to the Lord today and every day by *looking, living, and longing* for the person of Jesus Christ.

All Things Considered

(Psalms 8:1–4, Matthew 6:29–31,
Haggai 1:4–8, and Romans 8:18)

When I consider the heavens
And survey the earth,
I am overwhelmed by all I see.
But what marvels me most of all
Is that you are mindful of me!

When I consider the lilies, the grass,
And the birds of the air,
I am humbled by what I see.
Because Solomon, in his greatest glory,
Could not compare to the glory of these.

When I consider my ways,
My thoughts, my words, my deeds,
I am ashamed by what I see.
Because I have not glorified my God,
After all he has done for me.

When I consider the cross
And my savior dying for me,
My soul fills with love overflowed like a sea.
Because I see hanging there
The one who died for me.

When I consider the sufferings of our present time,
The evil, despair, and pain,
I am discouraged by what I see.
But then I am reminded of the glory,
Which will be revealed, when Christ in his glory
we shall see.

Having considered all these
And pondered to the end,
I know that my life is in God's hands.
Because from the very beginning,
When before I was known, he considered me to
be one of his!

Along for the Ride
(Psalms 23 and 1 Corinthians 14:20)

I can remember as a little boy getting into the car on Friday afternoon and leaving out to go to a softball tournament. This was the case for many weekends throughout the summer, and because of it, I have had the opportunity to go to many different places.

As a child, I sometimes imagined how it was that Daddy knew exactly how to get where we were going. I remember one time asking him how he knew where he was going. And he said by way of a map, road signs, and memory. I never worried whether we were going to get there and back home again. I believed that Daddy knew what he was doing and where he was going.

This is the essence of childlike faith. If ever we need to become like little children, it's now. With so much uncertainty and the future of the country weighing in the balance, we really don't know where we are heading as a country. There are many preachers and prophets who are prophesying and saying this and that is going to happen, and they may be right. Only time will tell. Until then, we just have to trust that, just as my daddy was driving the car knowing where he was going and what he was doing, it is the same way with us as children of God. We just have to trust him!

God has given us the road map of the Bible, the signs of the times, and the memory of where he has brought us from, with the truth that he, like my earthly father, will bring us home someday. We know as Christians that heaven is that home, but just how God's providence will get us there, we are not sure. He is surely preparing a place for us and will come again and receive us unto himself. Until then, we stay patient and focused until he comes, praying even so, "Come, Lord Jesus!"

So this brings me to our Scripture text. Paul said that we are to be children in malice and adults when it comes to spiritual maturity. These are the two necessary ingredients to childlike faith. As evil abounds and darkness sets in even deeper, we will find ourselves walking in the valley of the shadow of death that our culture is experiencing right now. But remember Christ is with us, and his rod and staff will be a comfort to us. Mercy and goodness will follow us all the days of our lives, and we will eventually make it home where we will dwell in the house of the Lord forever.

That good shepherd is Christ our Lord. Peter tells us to follow in his steps. I don't know where this country is going in the near future, but what I do know is I am determined to follow Jesus through it. It is just one of many destinations that we must go through on our journey of life and to heaven. So let us not fear, despair, or grow weary in well doing. He will take us through it and bring us home!

Read and meditate on 1 Peter 1:21–25.

Are You He?
(Matthew 11:1–11)

"Are you who you say you are?" That is the question that John sent with his disciples to Jesus prior to his execution. It's hard to believe that the forerunner of Christ had such doubts and fears. After all, it was John who heard the voice of God the Father say, "This is my beloved Son in whom I am well pleased," and witnessed the coming of the Holy Spirit in the form of a dove at Jesus's baptism in the Jordan River. After believing by faith, witnessing what he witnessed, and hearing what he heard, he still in his moment of despair asked, "Are you the one, or is there another?"

If I had been John the Baptist, I would not have wanted this recorded. But the Holy Spirit moves on the gospel writers to do so for our admonition. Whether we want to admit it or not, we also experience doubt and fear from time to time, especially in the wake of death, sickness, suffering, and loss. That's when the devil begins to assail upon the mind to blind you and me to faith.

There are three things we learn from this incident.

First, the men and women in the Holy Scripture, whom we tend to place on a higher level, had their struggles and doubts. It reminds me of a saying from Evangelist Keith Speed, "Man at his best and the best of men have faults and failures, and we dare not build a tabernacle for man." They were human with like passions such as we have.

Second, when John had this doubt, he didn't not try to fight it alone; he took it to Jesus. When we are struggling with faith, we can go to him who gives us faith and grants us that extra measure of faith in time of need.

> Have we trials and temptations?
> Is there trouble anywhere?
> Our precious savior,
> He is still our refuge.
> Take it to the Lord in prayer.

Third, Jesus did not rebuke John for his doubt but encouraged him in it. In fact, he commends John on his faithfulness to the purpose for which he was born. Our Lord knows when to rebuke and when to encourage. Here, he encourages one of his own in his time of imprisonment. Worry, fear, and discouragement are all prisons in which God's people are confined to from time to time. And he knows how to deliver the godly out of them all.

Be honest and take your doubts and fears to the Lord. We serve a compassionate savior who remembers our frame and knows that we are dust. Matthew said, "A bruised reed he will not break and a smoking flax he will not put out." Jesus is always for us and not against us!

Is there another? No! Jesus is he which was, is, and is to come. What a friend we have in Jesus!

Read also Matthew 12:20.

Atonement (At-one-ment)
(Romans 5:11 and 8:29)

Paul uses the theological term "atonement" to describe our reconciliation and relationship with God. Atonement basically means that the conflict between God and man brought about by sin has been reconciled through Jesus's death on the cross. Our debt of sin has been paid and now, through the peace that comes by faith in Jesus Christ, makes us "at one" with God.

This has a twofold meaning for us as believers.

First, God is no longer our enemy. Paul said in Romans 5:10 that "we were enemies of God." Sin separates mankind from God, and because we loved darkness instead of the light, we kept rebelling and fighting against a loving and merciful God. But through the death of Christ on the cross and the outpouring of the Holy Spirit in whom Jesus said would convict and convince the world of sin, righteousness, and judgment to come, he draws all men unto himself through the preaching of the cross. By this, we are no longer enemies and are truly reconciled, being made at one with him.

Second, the atonement not only reconciles us to God but it also should conform us to the image of Christ. The atonement not only makes us at one with God in reconciliation but it should also make us so at one with Christ that his desire should be our desire. The oneness we have with him should be so close that nothing can divide it asunder. Our reactions are a response to his actions working in us. I believe this is what Paul meant in Philippians 2:13, that it is "God who works in you, both to will and to work for his good pleasure."

Rich Little was one of my favorite comedians when I was growing up. He was known as an impressionist. He could sound like many famous actors, entertainers, and politicians of his day. He would spend hours studying their voices and actions. When he did his acts, even those he mimicked would be astonished at how good he was.

This is a good lesson for us. The Bible teaches us that we are to conform (mimic) the person of Jesus Christ. How do we attain this? We study his words and his actions. Yet we have something even greater than the Bible. We have Christ living in us! In other words, if we would just surrender to his Spirit within us, we will find that it is he who does it all anyway. It is the supernatural working naturally in and through us.

Attraction, Not Distraction
(Psalms 142:1–2, 1 Timothy 2:1–4, and Colossians 4:5–6)

One thing that I have observed throughout this pandemic and election year is the amount of criticism that has been brought upon our political leaders from both the Left and the Right. I have concluded is that it is much easier to complain than to pray! It's much easier to criticize than to build up. We as Christians, in many ways, fight to keep sound doctrine and uphold moral living, but in the meantime, we are not biblical in our approach to rectifying the issues that are presented before us.

I honestly think that going on social media and assassinating the character of a political leader doesn't do them any harm but, at the same time, does a lot of harm to our Christian witness. To be honest with you, those politicians are not reading your posts or blogs anyway. At best, you are just venting and making yourself feel better while, on the other hand, making yourself or the church look like its unloving and uncaring in the process.

To stand for what is right is not only a biblical right, it is also a biblical mandate. But for it to be the most effective, it must be done the biblical way. When I grew up playing sports, I was bad to trash-talk. Many times, in the process, I was the one ending up looking like a fool when it was all said and done. Trash-talking may have its place on the field or court, but not in the church.

So what should be the church's attitude and approach in times like these?

First, if we are going to complain, let us do as the psalmist and "offer our complaint unto the Lord." Our words may not change a thing, but our prayers can.

Second, we need to do as Paul encouraged Timothy to do and "offer up supplications, prayers, and intercessions, and giving of thanks, for all men; for kings, and for all in authority." Why? "So that we made lead a quiet and peaceable life in all godliness and honesty." From this, we learn to pray for those in authority who abuse their power and to be thankful for those we have that are good and godly leaders.

Lastly, when we are drawn into the conversation, we must strive in every way to do as Paul said, "Our speech be with grace, seasoned with salt." Let us speak honestly but also gracefully that we may "be ready to give a reason for the hope we have in Christ with gentleness and respect" (1 Peter 3:15). The Bible teaches us that we are to respect a person not for what they believe but for the fact that they are human beings made in the image and likeness of God.

We must strive to be like our Lord in our dealings with others. Like him, the church should be more of an attraction and not a distraction!

Be Patient
(James 5:1–8)

There are many paradoxes in life. I think one of the most ironic ones is to wait forty-five minutes in line at a *fast-food* restaurant! Living in a fast-food, fast-internet, fast-car, and fast-travel age, we have lost one of the most critical attributes of the early church: *patience*!

We have been groomed in our high-tech culture to get what we want when we want it. Through Amazon Prime, we can get our orders in one or two days, and through online grocery orders, we can pick up, not even having to get out of the car at some places. By this, we are able to avoid long lines and price checks, only just to hurry along to rush through the next task of the day. This lifestyle has stripped us of one of the most reoccurring teachings throughout the Scripture: *patience*.

James is addressing the church in one of its most afflicted times. Since many Christians had been scattered, they were having to take the available jobs that many didn't want. A lot of these jobs were in agriculture or crafting, and because of their desperation, many of their bosses were taking advantage of them, withholding some of their wages. They worked hard for next to nothing, and they cried out to God for justice.

This was James's response to them from the Holy Spirit: "Be patient!" He reminds them of the story of Job and talks about how patient Job was in his affliction. He reminds them that the Lord was "pitiful" unto Job and that his later end was better than the beginning. Then he says that when the Lord comes again, he will bring truth and justice with him and make things right.

Today we are experiencing the trying of our patience. Many of us feel that we have been cheated, robbed, or mistreated. There have been politicians who have manipulated their way into power and corporations that have gouged and have taken advantage of both employees and consumers in a time of crises. There have been governors who have shut down places of worship while allowing bars, strip joints, and ABC stores to remain open. It is really unfair, and it seems that "no one calls for justice" (Isaiah 59:4). But there are people who are crying out for justice, and it is not seen in protest in the streets but is heard by God from his people in prayer closets and prayer meetings.

I remind you today what Abraham said to God, "Will not the judge of all the earth do right?" (Genesis 18:25). God is a just God, and he will bring justice upon all who act unjustly. We just have to be patient and wait on him. How do we do this?

- We establish our hearts (verse 8).
- We keep looking for Christ to come (verse 8).

"Establish" in this sense means to "plant down." Or as we say in the South, "Hunker down." In times like these, we need to focus on allowing our roots to grow deeper so that we will not falter under the false winds of doctrine and deception that is destroying our culture today. We also need to let our roots grow downward that we may bear fruit upward. *Patience* is a fruit of the Spirit.

With all the injustice, lies, deceit, and blasphemy in our culture today, we have to accept that not all will receive recompense in this life. But when Christ comes again, he will judge both the living and the dead, and each will receive their just payment for their wickedness and rebellion toward God and his people.

Jesus said, "In your patience possess ye your souls" (Luke 21:19). Let us do as James said and "be patient therefore brethren until the coming of the Lord" (verse 7). "For yet a little while, and he that shall come will come, and will not tarry!" (Hebrews 10:37).

Beware of False Prophets
(Matthew 24:4–5, 11, and 24)

As we are living in confusing times, it seems that many Christians are adding to the confusion instead of bringing clarity. I am reminded of what King Zedekiah asked Jeremiah the prophet in time of confusion and chaos, "Is there any word from the Lord?" (Jeremiah 37:17). Although Zedekiah never really cared much about what God had to say up to this point, now in a time of desperation, he is ready to listen. I think people today are ready to listen, but from many church leaders, there is not a clear and biblical message coming forth.

Jesus was sharing with his disciples prophetic answers to their questions of when the temple would be destroyed. One sign that Jesus emphasized the most was false Christs and false prophets. The three years prior to the fall of Jerusalem was filled with chaos and confusion, and many self-proclaimed prophets and messiahs were taking advantage of the situation. All the prophecies and promises came to nothing, and instead of listening to Jesus and fleeing Jerusalem, many perished or were enslaved during the siege.

The point is that they should have listened to Jesus's words. In our time of chaos and confusion, we need to do the same! There have been many self-proclaimed prophets over the last year that prophesied things concerning the pandemic and election. All that it has led to have been mounting conspiracy theories, failed prophecies, and false hope. The result is that many are now turning away from the church instead of running to it.

Peter said that we have a "more sure word of prophecy" (1 Peter 1:19) that we need to take heed to. That sure word is the Bible. Isaiah said, "If they speak not according to this word, it is because there is not light in them" (Isaiah 8:20).

The Bible is the standard by which we judge whether someone is prophesying in the name of the Lord or whether they are a self-proclaimed charlatan trying to steal the spotlight to build up his own ministry. He may build himself up, but at the same time, he may be letting some down and leading others astray. Biblical prophecy must be interpreted in the light of how Jesus and the writers of the New Testament interpreted them. Many things that have been proclaimed about the end times in the last few decades have simply not come to pass.

So I want to encourage you to "seek out the book of the Lord and read" (Isaiah 34:16). But just don't read it. Read it prayerfully so that you will not be deceived and be ready, for "the Son of man will come in a time that you think not!" (Matthew 24:44).

The Christian as a Peacemaker
(Matthew 5:9)

"One nation under God, indivisible…"

It was the vision of our founding fathers that this nation, made up of what have become fifty states, be always be united. It has already endured one trial of division during the civil war, and now it faces its biggest trial since then. We are so divided as a nation today between Republicans and Democrats, nationalists and globalists, and Conservatives and Liberals. And even in the churches between denominations, conservative theology and liberal theology, and moral gospel and social gospel.

I am reminded of the words of Jesus as he said, "A house divided cannot stand."

So what is the role of Christianity in this? What are we to do in times like these? The answer is to make peace. We are to be peacemakers in a nation that is at war with itself politically, racially, socially, and spiritually.

In the Greek, Peace (Eirene) means to enter into the volatility and not abstain from it. The tendency today is to try to stay out of the fighting. Jesus tells us to get involved and help bring resolve. This is what Jesus did when, through the incarnation, came into the world to bring peace between God and man. Paul said in Romans 5:1, "We have peace with God through our Lord Jesus Christ."

So first of all, peace begins in the heart, mind, and heart. Once we have made peace with God, then we have to make peace with our neighbor. All this peacemaking begins through prayer and repentance and seeing others not for as they are but who they are being made into, the image of God.

Our role is not to be as spectators but innovators, motivators, and arbitrators and "enter bravely into the conflict to declare God's terms and make a man whole." Let us not be as King Saul who, for forty days, listened to the threats of Goliath, hoping he would get tired and go away. No, let us be as David and address all these issues that are threatening to destroy our country in the name of the Lord.

If God can bring peace and reconciliation between himself and fallen man, how much more through the gospel and the ministry of reconciliation, which has been given to the church? Can it bring peace to our families, churches, and communities?

It can be done and must be done for our survival. And it must be done in Jesus's name. Ask him to make you a peacemaker today!

Read 2 Corinthians 5:17–20 for future encouragement.

See Helps Ministries Word Studies.

Called to Be Saints
(Romans 1:7)

Paul is writing what is considered by many to be his masterpiece to the church in Rome. Wait a minute! There is a church in Rome? Looking at how this one-time great civilization had fallen into such a state of depravity and debauchery, it's hard to imagine that God would have a church in Rome. Yet he did, and because of it, we have one of the most in-depth description of the gospel and its influence on the lives of those who believe.

As Paul addresses this church in his introduction, he reminds the Roman believers of their calling. They are called to be saints.

Right in the midst of all the corrupting influences, they were called to be salt and light. The holy calling, which is what the word "saint" means, was to be one that was separate from the lifestyles that were defining Rome while, at the same time, defining what is meant to be a follower of Jesus. The Greek word is "*hagios*," which means to set apart for God. In others words, we consecrate ourselves to be exclusively his, accomplishing his will and purposes in this life as he is preparing us for the eternal life with him.

Today, you and I have this same calling. America has, in many ways, become like Rome of old. We too, which at one time was a great civilization, have now fallen into a state of depravity and debauchery, and yet the challenge remains for you and me to live holy and separated lives unto God. You mean that God has a church in America? Yes, he does! And just as that ancient church in Rome was a model influence in its day, we too have that same obligation before us.

I offer up a reminder and a challenge for us today in our present culture from Peter who spent his last days in Rome before being put to death for his faith in Christ.

First, the reminder. Peter said in 2 Peter 2:9, "But ye are a chosen generation, a royal priesthood, a holy nation, a peculiar people; that ye should shew forth the praises of him who hath called you out of darkness into his marvelous light." Peter is reminding the believers scattered abroad that they are a nation of God's people who are to demonstrate light, holiness, and a unique lifestyle that bring praise to God.

Second, the challenge. Peter is encouraging the believers to stir up their pure minds and to remember that they have been purged from their sin. Then he challenged them by saying, "Wherefore the rather, brethren, give diligence to make your calling and election sure: for if ye do these things, ye shall never fall" (2 Peter 1:10).

We too have that same calling and election.

Is it possible to have a church in America that is separate and holy unto the Lord? Yes, not only is it possible but it is also a necessity, and God has brought us into his kingdom for such a time as this. In times like these, may we be up to the challenges before us and, by God's grace, represent him well in a fallen culture.

Can Anything Good Come Out of Nazareth?
(John 1:44–46)

What wonderful news has been expressed in our text, especially to a Jewish man. The Messiah has come! You would think that Nathanael's response would be one of joy and relief. But he allowed his prejudice and contempt for a town and people to cause him to be skeptical.

Nazareth indeed held no great reputation in Jesus's day. It was known for its sinfulness and immorality. Can a good, honest, long-awaited deliverer come out of a horrible, desolate place?

In one sense, it is a fair question but one that must not be addressed with doubt. When we remember that with God all things are possible, not only do we know he can bring good out of good situations but also good out of bad situations.

Paul tells us, in the much-quoted verse of Romans 8:28, "All things work together for good." These "all things" are made up of good things, bad things, big things, and small things. There have been revivals that came about as a result of war. There have been conversions that came about through natural disasters. There have been great spiritual and world leaders that have done great things that have come out of a bad home life. There have been great churches formed that have resulted from disagreements and splits. Most of all, there have been places in the world where the gospel has been carried to because of persecution.

You may be in a present situation right now that is bad—a bad job, a bad relationship, or just a bad day. Your response may be as Nathanael's: "Can anything good come out of this?" I will respond to your question as Philip did, but in a slightly different way: "Wait and see." Living in a world gone bad produces evil and suffering. But God, through these trials and tribulations, brings forth patience, experience, and most importantly hope.

The greatest good that ever came forth out of bad situation was when Jesus died on the cross. What man meant for bad, God meant for good. It is the goodness of God that leads bad men and women to repentance!

Change
(Colossians 1:6)

One word that we hear a lot today in culture is "change." Social justice advocates want change. They want equality, justice, and reform. Christians want to change worship, doctrines, and standards to meet the demands of culture instead of trying to lead it in the ways of the Lord. Believe it or not, I am an advocate for change. Not the change that I have mentioned above but the type of change that comes from preaching and believing the gospel.

The New Living Translation of our text reads like this: "This same good news that came to you is going all over the world. It is bearing fruit everywhere by changing lives, just as it changed your lives from the day you first heard and understood the truth about God's wonderful grace."

The purpose of the gospel is not just to redeem but transform the one who receives it by faith unto a new life. It brings about a new heart, a new mind, and a new attitude toward God and sin. Paul said, "If any man be in Christ, he is a new creature, old things pass away and behold all things become new" (2 Corinthians 5:17).

Jesus gave a parable illustrating this new life. He said, "No one puts a new patch on an old garment. When it is washed, the patch will shrink and make the tear even worse" (Mark 2:21). In other words, the gospel is not about patching up the old life. It is about making a new life, a new man or woman.

So let us as Christians call for and be advocates of change, but do it the gospel way. Not by protest but by proclamation through our lips. Not by proselytizing but persuasion through our life.

Cheerful Tribulation
(John 16:33 and Revelation 5:1–14)

"Tribulation" and "cheer" in the same sentence? These two words on the surface do not seem compatible, much less found together in one sentence. Yet these are the very words of our Lord.

Jesus has just spent his last night giving final details about his approaching death and resurrection. He understood the reality of the evil in the world and the heart of man and how all that evil was to be thrusted upon him in atoning for the sins of the world. He also understood how that evil would then be thrusted upon them after his ascension and the coming of the Holy Spirit into the world to give life to his church. Although his honest critique of the world can be somewhat discouraging, he tells them to be of good cheer.

Why be cheerful? Because he overcame the world. When you look at the sufferings and death of Jesus, you see that it is rather breathtaking how he was beaten so brutally and yet survived to only then be nailed to the cross afterward. What is even more breathtaking is that the writer of Hebrews said he did it with joy (Hebrews 12:2)! He knew that his death was not a defeat but a victory. A victory not just for himself but also for his church.

When the disciples were arrested for preaching in his name, they were beaten and released with the command not to speak in his name anymore. Did this get them down? No! The Bible tells us that they left rejoicing because they had suffered for his name's sake. There is no greater honor than to identify with Jesus in suffering.

The faith that we hold is one that Jude said was worth fighting for (Jude 3). In every war, there are many battles. Some are won, and some are lost. There are many wounds, and most are left with some scars. Yet when the war is over and the victory is won, what a celebration of triumph!

That is why John, in his heavenly vision, sees Jesus as a lamb in the midst of the throne as one slain from the foundation of the world. The scars and wounds remain. But he also sees Jesus as the Lion of Judah. The one who has conquered death, hell, and the grave.

Jesus told his disciples that tribulation will be in the world, but be of good cheer. Why? Because he overcame the world. We will have our battles won and lost. We will have our wounds and scars, but we will also have our victory! Because all around the throne, there are a multitude of people from every nation, kindred, and tongue who overcame the world through Jesus Christ!

John said in Revelation 12:11 that the saints overcome the devil by:

- the blood of the lamb,
- the word of their testimony, and
- loving not their lives unto death.

After this in verse 12, he says to rejoice!

Thanks be unto God who gives us the victory through our Lord Jesus Christ. Be of good cheer today. If God is for us, who can be against us?

Don't Be Afraid
(Psalms 27:1 and John 8:12)

All of us, at one time or another, have taken a wrong turn and have gone down a road that was unfamiliar and uninhabited. There is an anxious and eerie feeling that sweeps over us, and we are looking for somewhere to turn around and go back. Imagine this feeling when there were no GPS systems or iPhones to help find your way back. As you are going down this deserted road, your mind begins to wander off to that horror movie you had previously watched, and you're waiting for a Jason, Freddy, or Michael to jump out at you. The sense of fear is overwhelming when traveling on dark unfamiliar roads.

At this time in history, we are traveling on one of those roads. We have made a wrong turn and are heading in unfamiliar and uncertain territory, and for many people, it has created a spirit of fear and weakness. What has gotten us to this point is not that we haven't had a GPS to guide us. We have turned it off! For some reason, we have gotten to the point to where we think we can move forward without God. Many of our leaders in churches and government feel that our road map, the Bible, is no longer relevant, or even worse, it has been so relevant that now it has become a form of hate speech to those who oppose its truths. Just because it tells us that we are sinners in need of a savior and that the lifestyles chosen today that are contrary to God's will and purpose for life are unfulfilling and lead to more pain and suffering, it has become a form of hate instead of help.

Jesus, who is our GPS, said that he is the way, the truth, and the life. And when you look at his life, it was one that was full of love and not hate. It was one that wasn't selfish but selfless, giving himself for us! Jesus said also that he is the light of the world and that those who do not follow him walk in darkness. At one time, we as a nation walked in the light of Christ and the gospel, but now we have made that wrong turn. And in turning, we have not turned away from a path but a person, the person of Jesus Christ.

So what does this mean for God's people? Are we to grope in the darkness of fear and despair? No! We walk in the light. We keep looking into the face of Jesus and onto the pages of his Word, for his Word is "a lamp unto our feet and a light unto our path" (Psalms 119:105). David said in our psalm that because God is our light and our strength, we have no reason to be fearful and discouraged. The godless and secular supermen and superwomen today may try to create fear and anxiety among the faithful in the Lord, but just like those horror characters of old, they too will come and go.

There have been many in the last two thousand years that were God's pallbearers. They made statements, like "God is dead" or "The Bible will be a dead book." But those men have come and gone, and Christ and his Word still rule and abide with us today. Jesus said that because he is the light of the world, they who follow him will walk in the light of life. So what do we have to fear? Of whom do we need to be afraid? I am reminded of the words of Jesus when he said, "Fear not them who are able to destroy the body, but fear him who is able to destroy both the body and soul in hell" (Luke 12:4–5). It sounds to me like the modern atheist and secularist are the ones who should be afraid!

Don't Get Stuck
(Genesis 19:1–26)

2020 was a year unlike any other year in most of our lifetimes. Every year has those one or two events that stick out and somewhat defines that particular year. But 2020 was so eventful that it will be considered most likely as a paradigm shift in human history. In other words, it will be a fixed point of reference for the decades following that will have influenced world events.

The tendency is to look back at the events that happened and to think how they affected our daily lives. For the most part, the impacts were negative and have had their emotional, psychological, and, for some, spiritual impacts. The challenge for us as God's people is not to look back but to look forward.

In our scriptural text, the angels told Lot and his family just one thing: "Don't look back!" They were to look up to a higher place that they were leading them to, which were the mountains. After receiving the warning to flee because of God's impending judgment on Sodom, Lot was somewhat slow and reluctant to pack his things and go. There are a few of lessons here to be learned.

First, in Lot's reluctance, the angels had to hasten him to get ready. In other words, there was this fervent persistence from the angels to hurry up. Why did he delay? It is possible he had some ties to some things in Sodom that were meaningful to him.

Second, the angels had to literally pick Lot and his family up and carry them to the gate of the city. Was it unbelief, or did they think they had more time? Who knows? I think both reasons could apply.

Finally, Lot's wife looked backed! It appeared that she was heading to safety, but in her heart, she was still in Sodom.

The application for us is not to look back to 2020 and get stuck there. Let us not dwell on those events that impacted our lives in a negative way to keep us from going where God wants us to go, which is a higher place. Don't let traditions that were affected cause us from reaching out into new things while still proclaiming the same message. Let us not be slow to react to the call of being prepared, for the Day of the Lord is at hand. Christ's second coming is nearer than we think. Finally, let us not dwell on our sins and failures that we had, but let us look to that hill called Calvary where Christ paid the price for our sin.

Lot's wife, in looking back, was turned into a pillar of salt and remains in the same place from where she looked back. Don't get stuck in 2020 by constantly looking back. Look forward, look up, and let God lead you to a higher place in him!

Encourage Yourself in the Lord
(1 Samuel 30:1–18)

David is having a bad day! The Amalekites are out to kill him. The Philistines don't trust him. His wives have been kidnapped along with the wives of his soldiers. His city had been burned down and last but not least, his army blames him for it and wants to stone him. I can only sum it up in the words of Charlie Brown, "Good grief!" Yet the Bible says, "David encouraged himself in the Lord."

Discouragement is a powerful tool of the devil. It blinds the mind to faith and can cause one to become weak and lose heart. We all have experienced it in one way or the other, and how precious are those words from a pastor, teacher, parent, or friend in those times. That timely sermon, daily devotion, or maybe a song that seems to come at the right time can be very uplifting and give one the strength to go on. But what about those days when the phone doesn't ring, you don't receive a text, your favorite song isn't played, or the sermon just doesn't resonate with your problem? It is then that you have to muster up enough strength to "encourage yourself in the Lord."

David had, at many times, been a source of strength and encouragement to his men and eventually to his country through his faith in God, through the songs he played, and the psalms he wrote. We still draw encouragement from these today. We have all been used by God in the past as an instrument of encouragement to help others. But the hardest ones to encourage the most are ourselves.

I think the secret to it all is that we have to remember that God is always with us and never abandons us, even when our faith is weak. David's wives may have been taken. His possessions may have been taken. And even his army wanted to abandon him. But he knew that God would never leave him or forsake him. It was through prayer and a renewed confidence in God that David got everything back that was lost.

It may be as we move forward into this new year that there will be many more changes and challenges ahead of us, and they may cause us to be discouraged and lose heart. But every day, we must encourage ourselves by remembering that God is the same and is a constant in an ever-changing world. He is with us. He is for us. And most of all, he is within us. In whatever situation may take hold of us, it takes hold of him as well because when it gets us, it gets him too. It gets the whole package!

Feeling Let Down, Look Up
(2 Corinthians 4:8–18 and Hebrews 11:24–27)

Over the past few months, there has been a big letdown in our expectations concerning our country. It feels as though the breath has been taken out of us and no life remains in us. If we feel this way as a result of an election, I can't imagine how Paul felt when he was more than let down. He was beat down, put down, brought down, and cast down. I would say he was down in the dumps!

But really, he wasn't. Paul probably had far more disappointments than we will ever have. And yet he remains positive, uplifted, and hopeful. Why? Because he had focus! He did not look at the things that were seen, but he looked at the things unseen. He did not put his trust in temporal things but in the things that were eternal. In other words, he focused on the things that were already said and done. Things already completed through Jesus Christ and the cross, resurrection, ascension, and his meditation in heaven at God's right hand.

- Having been afflicted, he did not allow those afflictions to crush his spirit.
- Having been confused, he never lost focus.
- Having been persecuted, he realized he was sharing in the sufferings of Christ.

51

- Having been struck down, he knew that death did not have the final word.

You see, we die a little every day. The outward man perishes, but inside, we live a little more every day. The inward man is renewed. This renewal comes from feasting on the Word of God which fuels our faith, hope, and love and constantly reminds us of the promises that we have in our risen Lord.

There are many things that are letting us down right now, but these are temporary things. I believe what God is saying to us is to look up. Look unto Jesus. Do as Moses did when he refused to be called Pharaoh's son and chose to suffer affliction with the people of God. He saw that the treasures in Egypt were temporal. The Bible tells us that Moses endured by seeing him who is invisible.

We may not see him, but he is the God who is there! It is he who is the lifter of our heads and will lift us up when we have been let down.

Four Pillars of Enduring Faith
(Romans 12:12)

In this passage of the Scripture, I think we have the remedy for surviving a pandemic. If there has been anything that has sapped our joy, left us in despair, tried our patience, and challenged our prayer life, it has been the coronavirus. But Paul tells us that we need to remain joyful, hopeful, patient, and prayerful, for these are the strengths of a Christian.

Let's look at each of these briefly.

Rejoicing in hope. The joy and hope we have is not dependent on tangible things or situations. They are rooted in the person of Jesus Christ. Paul said, "Rejoice in the Lord always, again I say rejoice!" He also said of hope that we "look for the blessed hope and glorious appearing of our great God and savior Jesus Christ." Notice again that these two, joy and hope, are grounded in the person of Christ and in his second coming.

Being patient in tribulation. Jesus said that it is in being patient that we "possess our souls." Patience means to endure hardship without complaint. Like Job, we have to be able to say in whatever has been lost in this time, "The Lord gives and the Lord takes away; blessed be the name of the Lord."

Continuing in prayer. Jesus said that men ought to always pray and not faint. Prayer keeps us from growing tired and weary, keeping our focus on the Lord and not our circumstances. It was through the widow woman's continual coming to the unjust judge that she was finally avenged of her adversary. Jesus asked the question, "Will the son of man find this kind of faith on the earth when he comes again?"

The time just before the return of Christ will be a time of testing. These four things in which Paul mentions here are pillars that will uphold God's people in trying times, such as the times we are living in now. Just like the four men who brought the palsied man to Jesus, these four Christian attributes of joy, hope, patience, and prayer will guide us through to Jesus and sustain us in this time of paralysis due to COVID-19.

From Bitter Days to Brighter Days
(Isaiah 40:31 and Galatians 6:9)

My cross is so heavy!
I'm tired!
I'm weary!
I am ready for it to come to an end.
I am tired of fighting, though I have fought a good fight.
I have finished my course, though a rugged one it has been.
I have kept the faith, a faith worth keeping.
I am tired!
I am weary!
I am like Christ in the garden, wanting this cup to pass from me.
I am praying for another way, a better way, an easier way.
But nevertheless, I know there is no other cup, no better cup, no easier way.
So I pray not my will then but thy will be done!
In accepting this cup, I am still tired but refreshed.
I am still weary but renewed.
I know that darker times are to come.
Yet there is light at the end of the tunnel.
I am spent!
I am discouraged!
I feel like the psalmist when he said, "No one cares for my soul."

But then, in a moment, in the depth of my despair,
I am reminded of a sermon from a man of God:
"Life is hard, but God is good!"
Yes! God is good! He is great!
And great is his goodness and mercy toward us all!
I am strengthened in knowing that he is for us!
And if he is for us, who can be against us?
What is this? I feel as though I have gotten a second wind.
I am not tired!
I am not weary!
I am not weak!
I am not discouraged!
I feel strong!
I am strong!
Not in my own strength but in the strength of the Lord!
I take up my cross. Though rugged, it doesn't feel as heavy!
I have learned that "they who trust in the Lord, he will renew their strength.
He shall mount them up on eagle's wings.
They shall run but not be weary.
They shall walk and not grow faint."
I know that we live in bitter days.
But better days are coming.
We live in dark times, but a brighter time is on the horizon.
There is coming a new day, with a new sun.
A day when the sun of righteousness will arise with healing in his wings.
A day when there will be no more need of the sun, for Jesus will be the light.
So let us not be weary in well doing.
For in due season, we will reap if we faint not!

Get Your Mind Right
(1 Peter 1:13)

I have been accused, at times, of being a scatterbrain. It is usually in those moments when I have so much on my mind that I can't really think or function. Many times, it comes from having too many responsibilities, unexpected turns, or just worrying about various things that are out of my control.

In a technological age, you would think that we would be more organized, more on top of things, and less stressed from the electronic advancements that have been offered to us. But it is quite the opposite. Because of these things, we have more responsibilities, more news, and more information than we have ever had before. Along with this comes more demands, which equates to even more responsibilities. And the next thing we know, time has flown by, and we are exhausted.

More than this, we have a pandemic, an undecided election, threats of further shutdowns, and the holidays! All these things are causing us to be distracted and take the focus off what is really important, which is our looking unto Christ every day for his grace and his return.

If there was ever a time when this verse was applicable to us, it is now. Peter said, "Gird up the loins of your mind." To "gird up" means to pull everything together that is loose so that nothing can hinder your movement. In this case, it tells us that all our scattered thoughts, worries, and fears that hinder us from being focused on the task at hand and that great event of Christ's second coming need to be harnessed. In other words, we need to get our minds right!

He also tells us to be sober. To "be sober" means to be aware of your surroundings by being able to think clearly. Worry, fear, and doubt can be a type of spiritual drunkenness that causes us to be disillusioned and deceived.

Finally, he tells us to hope. If our minds are girded and sober, then it helps us focus on the reality of the hope that we have in Christ in a hopeless world.

Through all this, we will see that God's grace will be sufficient for us. And because it can never be exhausted, we have the promise that there will be enough to supply us until the end.

God behind the Scenes
(Jeremiah 29:10–14 and Zechariah 4:10)

Sometimes God's work is so evident that it is seen, and the devil is working behind the scenes. Then there are those times when the devil's work is so evident, yet God is working behind the scenes. Nevertheless, both God and the devil are always at work.

Jeremiah is sharing a prophecy of a time when it seems that God is hidden. He warns of the coming Babylonian judgment and says that they will be enslaved for seventy years. He tells them that God has good plans for them to give them "a future and a hope" (verse 11 ESV). But before then, it will appear that the devil is having his day and that God is hidden.

Jeremiah tells the people that God is not hidden and has not forsaken his people. He proclaims that God will be there but that they will have to look for him. And if the look for him, they *will* find him. This is the challenge for God's people in difficult times. It is so easy for us to focus on the negative and to gaze upon all that is wrong. This is the natural tendency because evil is having its day. It is more evident than the good things that are happening. But nevertheless, it is spiritually important for us to seek God and find him. And at this moment, we may not see him on the stage but working behind it.

This present time that we are in is just a period of history that is a part of God's great story and redemptive plan. Shakespeare said, "All the world's a stage." And at this stage in history, we see that the enemy is on the scene. But there is another scene and another act to come in which God will quench the power of evil and bring judgment upon the ungodly. The script has been written, and we patiently wait for it to be played out. In the meantime, we must look at the small things that God is doing, and that comes from prayer and a pure heart that sees God in all things.

There was another point in Israel's history when they were under the power of evil. It was in Elijah's time when Ahab and Jezebel were king and queen. Idolatry was rampant, and injustice was prevailing. It had not rained in three and a half years. Finally, after God had brought fire down upon the prophets of Baal and Israel cried, "The Lord he is God," Elijah went to pray for rain. After praying seven times, his servant saw a cloud about the size of a man's hand. This was all that Elijah needed. It wasn't a big sign, but nevertheless, it was a sign to let him know that rain was coming (1 Kings 18:41–45).

Sometimes God does big things, and then at other times, he does small things. Zechariah 4:10 tells us not to despise the day of small things. Don't overlook those small blessings, little acts of kindness, or simple words of encouragement and hope. Seek God today. And when you seek him, you will find him when you search for him with all your heart!

God Cares
(Psalms 142 and 1 Samuel 22:1–5)

Some of the best songs, poetry, or paintings come from those who are experiencing disappointments, failures, or discouragement. It is almost as if God has to squeeze us to bring out the best in us. This is why this psalm is one of the most touching and encouraging of all the ones that David wrote.

The title says that it is a Maschil of David while he was in the cave. The word "Maschil" means instruction. So it is a song of instruction to those who are experiencing loneliness, pain, and despair. The cave is called Adullam, which means "the place of the squeeze." If you read the background story found in 1 Samuel 22:1–5, you will learn that David was not really alone but was in the company of those who were in distress, in debt, and discontented. It also says that he was their captain. I can imagine, as David wanders off to be by himself, it is then that he receives the inspiration to write this psalm.

You would think that with so many people within this gathering, they would be able to lean on one another and draw strength from one another, but the depth of their despair had really brought them so low that it made David feel:

- overwhelmed (verse 3),
- trapped (verse 3),
- lonely (verse 4),
- restless (verse 4), and
- that nobody cared for him (verse 4).

At Adullam, David had been squeezed so much that he felt dry spiritually and left for dead. He thought he had been abandoned.

Throughout these unprecedented times, I think we all have experienced at least one, if not all, of these emotions. We too are feeling the squeeze and the pressure of having to make changes and decisions that take us out of our comfort zones.

- Daily routines have been disrupted due to the decision made to conduct public school virtually.
- There have been people who have lost their jobs and are having trouble making ends meet.
- There are so many unhappy people that suicides, divorce, and mental illness are at an all-time high.
- There is so much political unrest and uncertainty in our country that is creating panic and chaos.

So what is the remedy? What is the cure? David, after pouring out his complaint in the first four verses, comes to verse 5 and remembers God. Not only does he remember God, he remembers that God cares! He said, "Lord, bring me out of this prison and take me to that place where I can praise you" (verse 7). God cared for David so much that he sent the prophet Gad to him and told him to go to Judah. Judah means praise (1 Samuel 22:5).

The Lord Jesus Christ came out of the tribe of Judah. The application is to go to Jesus today with your concerns. He really cares for your soul. He not only says it but he demonstrated it by taking all your sins, sicknesses, and sufferings upon himself on the cross. Your cave was his cross. And because he arose from the dead, he too will bring out those who are imprisoned in the tombs of their despair.

Cast all your care upon him, for he cares for you!

God Has Not Forgotten
(Isaiah 49:15–16)

As a pastor, I have always strived to be as mindful of every person and of everyone's situations as much as possible. I have found that the older I get, I need to write down various prayer request, appointments, and needs. In fact, thanks to modern technology, I put these notes and appointments in my reminder app to remind me at certain times and on certain days. I do this because I love my congregation and care for them.

This is what God is saying through the prophet Isaiah in our Scripture. He loves you so much and is so mindful of you that he is saying, "I have you written in the palm of my hand. Your walls are continually before me." God is telling his people that when they are in a time of exile in Babylon, they will not be forgotten. He will eventually bring them back, not only to Israel but most importantly to himself.

Throughout this pandemic, we feel like we have been exiled. We have found ourselves living much different lives than before. For a lot of people, it doesn't feel like the same country we were living in just a year ago. Some, due to high-risk health issues, are not getting out and about and are experiencing loneliness, boredom, and maybe despair. Some people's lives haven't changed that much. But still with limited access to various materials, food, entertainment, sporting events, and gyms, it has disrupted their everyday way of living. Even churches have had to adjust and be creative in how we have worshipped.

The point that I want to make this morning is simply this—a lot has changed, but God's love for you hasn't. His love is not some generalized love. He doesn't love you and me because he has to. He loves us because he wants to. He loves us so much that he is always thinking about us. Not only are our names written in his hand, the psalmist says that "our times are in his hands" as well. God is in control of this situation and just as a loving shepherd guides his sheep through dark valleys, our loving Lord will navigate us through these dark days and bring us to greener pastures.

The hands that we engraved in Isaiah's time became scarred in Jesus's time. When they drove the nails through the hands of Jesus, that was God's way of demonstrating his love toward us. After his resurrection, Jesus showed those scarred hands to Thomas. And when we see Jesus, as he extends his hands in welcoming us home, we too will see those scars.

I feel that this devotion is very personal today, and God wants you to know that in times like these, wherever you are in your walk with him, whatever you are feeling toward him, or whatever your spiritual or emotional state may be, he loves you and has not forgotten you. He had me to write this devotion to let you know, as your pastor, I love you and have not forgotten you either!

God Is Watching
(2 Chronicles 16:9)

Do you ever get the feeling that someone is watching you? You may look over your shoulder or turn back just to see if that is the case. In some instances, it is the case. The truth is that there is someone who is always looking at us, and it is God. He doesn't just look at us; he looks into us. Our text tells us that "his eyes go throughout the earth seeking out them that have a perfect heart towards him." Psalms 34:15 says that "the eyes of the Lord are upon the righteous." God is constantly watching over us. But it's more than just "watching over." He is literally "watching us."

I will illustrate it like this. When my kids were small, I would take them outside to play. As they were playing in the sand, I would take a book with me and study. Every now and then, I would look up to check on them and make sure they were all right. But then there were those times when I would put my book down and just watch them. It's amazing what you can learn about life from watching children.

God watches over us every moment of every day, but he also watches us. He knows where we are going and what we are doing, and he even looks at our hearts and knows why we are going and doing the things that we do. In many ways, this can give us the courage to live for him every day, knowing he is there to protect and shield us. But also, it teaches us to be careful with how we live our lives every day, not just publicly but also privately. Character and integrity are measured not by how we live when people see us but how we live when no one is looking. That is why God knows our true identity.

In the Gospel of John chapter 1, Nathaniel meets the long-awaited messiah, Jesus Christ. At first, he wondered if anything good could come out of Nazareth. His judgment was based on what he observed in his lifetime. But Jesus told Nathaniel that he was a man with no guile. Nathaniel responds, "How do you know me?" Jesus said, "I saw you when you were under the fig tree." The lesson here is that God is watching us, even when we are not looking for or at him.

Let us pray, as we not only live under his watch care but also his watching eye, that we may seek to have a perfect heart toward him. What is a perfect heart? It is a heart that is honest, sincere, and one that desires to be obedient. Think about how Jesus would describe you and me after observing us. Would he say the same about us as he did Nathaniel?

God Trusts You, Do You Trust Him?
(Job 2:1–10)

This is quite a dialogue taking place here in our text. It is one of those conversations that takes place in the mystical world around God's throne. The sons of God and Satan have appeared before God and must give an account unto him of their activities.

When God asked Satan, "From where have you come?"

Satan responds by saying, "From going to and fro on the earth and from walking up and down on it."

Then God says, "Have you considered my servant Job?"

Satan, the adversary and accuser, brings forth a false accusation by saying, "Skin for skin all that a man has he will give his life for but stretch out your hand and touch his bone and his flesh and he will curse you to your face."

God said, "Behold he is in your hand. Only spare his life."

There are two questions that I want to encourage you to reflect on today as you read this text.

First, we have heard about Job's faith in God. But what about *God's faith in Job*? Job was a man of integrity. The description of him from the mouth of God was that "there is none like him on the earth, a blameless and upright man, who fears God and turns away from evil." God knew Job's character and trusted him in a time of testing just as Job knew the character of God and trusted him. Job knew that God's grace and mercy was sufficient. The first thing we learn is that in our relationship with God, trust works both ways.

Second, *how do you respond to affliction*? What is your attitude when all of a sudden, things take a turn for the worst? There are given unto us two examples in this chapter:

- Job's wife's response: "Curse God and die."
- Job's response: "Shall we receive good from God and shall we not receive evil"? Then it says, "In all of this Job did not sin with his lips."

So which way do you respond to suffering and affliction? Job's faith or his wife's impatience and despair? Do you trust God as much as he trusts you? Remember the words of the apostle Paul to the Corinthians: "There is no temptation overtaken you that is not common to man. God is faithful, and he will not let you be tempted beyond your ability, but with the temptation he will also provide a way of escape, that you may be able to endure it" (1 Corinthians 10:13).

Remember, God is faithful, and he trusts you. The question is, do you trust him?

God's Indwelling Love
(1 John 3:17)

God not only has all the good, he is the very definition of good because there is none good but God (Mark 10:18)!

What if God who is good and possesses all things good had withheld the embodiment of goodness, Jesus Christ, from us? What if he were to shut up his bowels of compassion toward us? The answer to these two questions is simple. We would be lost and would die lost, coming under the terrible wrath and judgment of God.

But nevertheless, God saw that the world had a great need, and that need was redemption. The fullness of God's love dwelt in his incarnate Son, and as Mary's womb opened and Christ came forth, the most treasured gift of God was made known to the world.

John says that if the love of God dwells in us, then how can we close up our bowels of compassion? God's gift of love is not a mere emotion, but it is Christ himself abiding within us, wanting to express his love through our lives. This means we should see with the same eyes he sees with and hear with the same ears he hears with.

In the book of Matthew, Jesus looked out among scattered and lost sheep of Israel and had compassion on them (Matthew 9:36–38). Later on, he looked upon five thousand hungry men and told the disciples to feed them. With the bread and fish that they offered, along with his miracle working hands, all these men and their families were fed with much leftover (Matthew 14:15–21). I believe John had this in mind when he wrote this passage of Scripture.

Mother Teresa said, "No act of kindness, no matter how small, is ever wasted." The lesson for you and me this Advent season is that we need to look to give more than we receive. I pray, when we pass by one who is in need, that our bowels of mercy and compassion will burst open and that we will do a kind deed that may bring light and life to those who dwell in darkness.

Good Is Called Evil, Evil Is Called Good
(Isaiah 5:20)

I have read that when a pilot is flying in the clouds, he or she has to rely upon the instruments for position and direction. It is easy to get confused and not know whether you are up or down, going toward your destination or away from it. I have found recently that it is not only that way in flying but also in politics and religion.

Our country is experiencing an unprecedented time of confusion. We have lost our position and direction and are not using the instrument which our forefathers left for us to guide us and sustain freedom. That instrument is the Bible. It is the foundation by which the constitution and law was built upon. It was to be our moral compass. But because of a new system of belief that is very similar to an ancient but an ever-present and contemporary idea, we have become confused. It is called Babylon (confusion)!

One vision that was presented unto us for the future of our country has been referred to as enlightenment or advancement, although it is full of death, violence, hatred, immorality, and ungodliness. This had been referred to as light while the opposing view which promotes life, liberty, pursuit of happiness, decency, and respect has been referred to as dark. It is as Isaiah said, "Good is called evil and evil is called good."

Our culture has moved from the Judeo-Christian idea, which has an objective point of reference, to secular humanism, which is subjective and has no point of reference. In other words, "it is all sail and no anchor." It is blown about by every wind that blows or idea that comes along. This encourages instability. And what we see in our cities today concerning violence, bloodshed, and death is the outworking of that political philosophy.

What we need is stability. That implies the necessity of an anchor. We need something that will keep us grounded. Or to get back to our original illustration, we need an instrument to keep us located in the right position, moving in the right direction. This instrument is none other than the Bible!

As we move through these dark and challenging times, we can be assured of what is truly good and what is truly evil. The Bible defines these very clearly, and when we follow Bible truths, we will know the truth. And the truth will set us free. It is as the psalmist David said in Psalms 119:9, "Thy word is a lamp unto my feet and a light unto my path."

Jesus said, "There is none good but God" (Mark 10:18). Whatever the philosophy, ideology, or vision, if God is not in it, it's not good!

Gospel versus Politics
(Psalms 139)

What is the difference between the gospel and politics? This is a good question and one that needs to be answered. Some Christians do not see a difference, and that is why they are not effective witnesses for Christ. They identify more with a politician or a party than they do with Jesus. I do not doubt that both of these, Christianity and politics, do intersect at times, and most of the time, it is at the point of morality. Many of the controversial political issues today were biblical moral issues to begin with, but the church has been drawn into the political spectrum because of it instead of keeping the issues on biblical grounds.

Here is what I think the biggest difference is. Let's look at Socialism, for example. That seems to be the fastest-growing branch of political thought today. To give it some credit, it is concerned about the needs of humanity. It is driven by humanism, which do some good things in the world toward meeting the needs of mankind. Humanism can basically be summed up as "man is the measure of all things." My only question is which man? The biggest problem with this political thought is that it looks at humanity as a whole and not at individuals. Their policies are built around what is good for corporate humanity, not only in the present but generations to come. Therefore, for example, abortion is about the rights of women, not a woman or child. They claim also that abortion is a way to control overpopulation, therefore improving the conditions of the rapid deterioration of the environment due to climate change. Euthanasia is what is best for the healthcare system instead of the person needing healthcare. Heavy taxation is better for widespread poverty instead of the personal economic success of the individual having the freedom to be personally motivated and achieve his or her goals.

How is the gospel different? Jesus taught his disciples that they were to help the poor and needy, care for the fatherless and widows, and create a community of believers that look after other's needs before their own. There is no doubt that the modern church has failed in this and that government has had to shoulder the responsibility. The gospel is about "loving thy neighbor as thy self" and "doing unto others as we would have them to do unto us." When we embrace this, we understand that it's not about what is good for the country or the church. It is about each and every individual who is precious in the sight of God. This is what this psalm is describing: the uniqueness and importance of every single person.

I close by saying this. Jesus died, not for the whole world as much as he died for me! And he died for you! Each of us is fearfully and wonderful made and was formed in the womb by the very hand of God. That tells me that the individual—fetus, baby, toddler, man, woman, rich, poor, Black, White, Brown, etc.—is all precious and worth the life he laid down to save.

This is the church's creed, and when we get back to it, then we will see the gospel be the greater influence in our culture.

Happy to Be a Christian
(Acts 26:2)

Paul said, "I think myself happy!" I find this to be astonishing and very encouraging. Paul has been put on trial and is standing before King Agrippa, not for committing any crime but for being a Christian. And he is guilty as charged. If there was ever a time for him to be discouraged, it would be now because if Agrippa doesn't set him free, then he will have to stand before Caesar. Yet he is happy. He considers himself to be fortunate. Why? Because he is representing not himself in the court of law but Christ!

What a wonderful time it is to be a Christian in our world today. God has blessed his people to be his witnesses in a time when it is not very popular to be one. With the increase of secularization, atheism, and political correctness, the Christian life and biblical language is becoming more noticeable and increasingly offensive. It is as if Christians today are being tried in the court of public opinion. And my question to you and me is this: Would we be found guilty? Paul would eventually have to appeal to the highest court in the world at that time, which meant he had to give his defense before Caesar. It was there that he would be found guilty of being loyal to the lordship of Christ by not bowing to Caesar and recognizing him as lord.

What was the basis of Paul's conviction? He knew that he would stand before the judgment seat of Christ one day and give an account of how he lived his life before a watching world. In doing so, not only did he do it with conviction but also with joy!

It was Paul's joy that gave him the strength and power of his conviction. The Bible tells us that "joy of the Lord is your strength." When you and I as Christians have joy down in our hearts, we can endure any trial set before us and come out of it found guilty of being a faithful follower of Christ.

Jesus told his disciples that they would experience much sorrow and tribulation in the world, but he also said, "I tell you these things that your joy may be full" and to "be of good cheer for I have overcome the world" (John 16:24 and 33).

So let's consider ourselves today as Christians to be happy that God has chosen us for such a time as this to be his witnesses. Don't be discouraged or fearful, but pray for the Holy Spirit to strengthen your convictions and courage and pray for the opportunity to give a reason for why you believe (1 Peter 3:15).

Read and pray Psalms 144 today and focus on the last verse in that psalm that ends with "Happy is that people whose God is the Lord" (verse 15).

Having a Conscience
(Acts 24:16 and Titus 1:15–16)

There are many things that we could be praying concerning our country right now. Revival, the election, unity, justice, and healing. But I think that the most important thing to pray about concerning our country is the restoration of the conscience. You say why the conscience? Because that is where God speaks to us. If there is no conscience, then there is no hearing from God!

Paul said that he "exercises both day and night to have a good conscience toward God and man." He knew that the line between good and evil ran through the human heart, and what brought triumph over evil was the conscience's knowledge of the Word of God.

Today in our country, we have a generation that is void of a conscience. It is like what Paul said to Titus: "Unto the pure all things are pure: but unto them who are defiled and unbelieving there is nothing pure; even their mind and conscience is defiled. They profess that they know God but in works deny Him, being abominable, and disobedient, and unto every good work reprobate." The word "reprobate" means void of a conscience.

Another example is found in Romans 1:18–32. This is the condition of a culture who does not acknowledge God or, at most, has a distorted view of him.

For us, as God's people, the way we exercise having a good conscience is by reading and hearing the word with a prayerful attitude daily, asking God to give us a teachable spirit and ears to hear what the Spirit is saying to the church.

So I think that the most important prayer that we can pray right now is, first, for God to open the heart and conscience of our young people that they may be open to hearing the gospel and responding to its call to salvation. Then, second, that we would be ready to respond to that opening of the conscience with an answer for the hope we have in Christ with gentleness and respect.

Help, We Have Fallen
(2 Thessalonians 2:1–3, Revelation 2:1–7, and 2 Timothy 2:6)

"Help! I have fallen, and I can't get up."

We have all seen or heard this on television or radio. It is on one of the life alert commercials. When I was younger, I would poke fun at this. But then I fell in the shower a couple of years ago, and it is not funny anymore. Thank God I didn't get hurt, but as I look back, it happened so fast. And I could have broken a hip, leg, or shoulder.

Today, spiritually in our country, we have fallen, and we can't get up. What concerns me the most is that many people are not wanting to get up. There are politicians today who want to keep us down. They want us to remain in a broken state so that they can practice their ungodly ideas and promote their godless agenda.

How did we fall and fall so fast?

I want to be very sensitive here. It seems as though ever since the World Trade Center towers fell on September 11, 2001, we have not been able to rebuild our spiritual heritage in America. I think that after almost twenty years of reflecting on that moment, it was a sign of what was to come: our continual downward spiral and falling away from God.

The Bible records various falls throughout its record: the fall of Adam and Eve, the fall of Jerusalem to the Babylonians, the fall of Jerusalem to the Romans, the fall of society in Romans chapter 1, and the fall of the church of Ephesus from the first love.

All these falls have, one way or another, affected us. We see some of these in our contemporary churches and culture. But the one that I think is more contemporary and timelier to us today is that we have fallen away from the truth.

Our Scripture text tells us that before the Lord comes again that "that day shall not come except there come a falling away first and then the man of sin be revealed, the son of perdition." So what is this falling away? What does it consist of?

First, it is a falling away from the truth. It will be a time when deception will run rampant. Never before have I seen a time when people openly and unabashedly lie and have no shame about it.

Second, there are two types of "falling away" or also what we call apostasy.

There is theological apostasy, which means a turning away from the teachings of the Bible, Christ, and the disciples. Then there is moral apostasy, which means a deliberate turning away from Christ, a departure. Both of these are evident in our country today. Politically, we are turning away from God to secular ideas. Spiritually, the church has turned away from the moral teachings of Christ and the early church.

How do we get up? What is our life alert?

Prayer: Call upon the Lord in prayer (2 Chronicles 7:14).

Fall in love again: Remember, repent, and redo your first works is what Christ told the church of Ephesus when he pleaded for them to "return to their first love."

Stir up: Stir up the gift of God within us. We need to rouse ourselves up and get our senses together.

Meditate on these things today and let us make sure that we are *standing* on the foundation that we have in God through Jesus Christ.

If God Wills
(Romans 1:10 and James 4:13–15)

If you are like me, you try to live as organized as you possibly can in order to have some structure or a daily routine. Some of the most purchased items at the beginning of every year are planning apps and organizers to help bring that structure to our lives. We plan for the next day, next month, and next year and even step out on a limb and plan for retirement. One thing that I have learned is that you can plan all you want, but unforeseen things and events happen that throw the whole day or week out of order. Especially in turbulent times like these.

Paul wanted to go to Rome to help an already-established church by imparting unto to them a spiritual gift. As he opens this letter, he says that "he will come if it is God's will." There is no doubt that when you do an intense study of Paul's missionary journeys, you find out that it took much planning and organizing to accomplish this. He did not have a travel agent to help book ships and horses to get him from one place to the other. Careful coordination was essential in Paul's life to accomplish the purpose for which he was called.

But no matter how organized he was, there were those places and people that he wanted to see but didn't. He might have had them scheduled for a certain time or season, and when he went to depart, the Holy Spirit forbid him to go. Now he has a problem! The journey has been disrupted, and he now has to get out the maps and redo the logistics. You see, there is nothing wrong with planning our days, months, vacations, and retirements as long as we leave a few open times and dates for changes. We need to remember that God has plans for us, and we have to be discerning of his will and purpose in life.

I do not doubt that the disciples had big plans, but when they came to Christ, all that changed. Jesus said, "If you save your life [live according to your plans] you will lose it, but if you lose your life [surrender to the will of God] then you will find it" (Matthew 16:25). Paul in Galatians 2:20 said, "I am crucified with Christ, nevertheless I live, yet not I, but Christ lives in me: and the life which I now live in the flesh I live by the faith of the son of God..." What Paul is a saying is that he lives, but it's not his life but Christ's life in him.

James said, "What is your life?" Have you thought about that? What is your life all about? To the Christian, the answer is Jesus. James would go on say that "it is like a vapor that is here today and gone tomorrow." Life is brief, so we need to live it to the fullest. And the only way to do that is to live God's way, according to his will.

So let us do as James advised: "Don't say today or tomorrow we are going to such a city and continue there a year, and buy, and sell, and get gain." Remember what the writer of Hebrews said, "We have here no continuing city" (Hebrews 13:14). The only true plans we can make are to plan for eternity with Jesus by accepting him by faith. From there, we live and walk by faith, going wheresoever the shepherd and bishop of our souls lead us.

Insight
(Mark 6:35–52)

The New American Standard Bible says in verse 52, "For they had not gained any insight from the miracle of the loves, but their heart was hardened." I thought about this word insight. *Webster* defines insight as "the power or act of seeing into a situation; the act or result of apprehending the inner nature of things or of seeing intuitively." In others words, it means to be able to comprehend the inner nature of a person or thing. Having this situation laid out for us begs the question of how could the disciples have so much unbelief after having seen so many miracles? The answer being they did not understand the person of Jesus and the nature of his work.

Jesus performed miracles around the disciples every day. In our text, he had just performed two miracles that were on the level of beyond extraordinary: the feeding of the five thousand and calming the storm. And yet they still wondered and marveled that he should possess such power. I guess these things had become so commonplace in their daily routines that they overlooked the meaning and purpose of Jesus's ministry. I do believe that we should be astonished by what Christ does for his church on the level of the miraculous, not out of unbelief but of thanksgiving.

He does so many things for us each day, and we miss many of them due to our lack of acknowledging him. Many things he provides we take for granted, and when he does something on a greater level, then we respond like the disciples in wondering how he does this. What we need is insight in order to be able to apprehend his purpose in doing these things in our everyday lives.

God does not do these things for us just to show off. He does them for his glory and our benefit because he loves us and has taken on the responsibility of being our caretaker. He provides bread, clothing, finances, healing, and, above all, grace, mercy, forgiveness, and hope every day of our lives. We should never take credit for these things nor take them for granted, but glorify God in that he has "given unto us all things that pertain to life and godliness" (2 Peter 1:3).

You should take the time at the end of each day to meditate on the little miracles that God has done for you and in you that day. Pray that God will give you insight into what he is doing in your life. Do not miss out on the small things so that, when he does the big things, your heart won't be without understanding and hard like the disciples but thankful!

Into the Thick Darkness Where God Was
(Exodus 20:21)

John said of God, "In him is light, and there is no darkness in him at all." God is light, and his light is so majestic that to look upon him in his true essence would bring death. Even though there isn't any darkness in God, that doesn't mean he doesn't dwell in darkness. Our text tells us that "Moses drew near unto the thick darkness where God was."

I share this account with us because many are saying that we may be entering into one of the darkest periods of our nation's history. When we survey the list of things that are happening in our country, it does appear that there is an uncertainty about the future of this nation. Never has light and darkness been so laid out before us and contrasted as it has been in this election year. The pandemic, protests, riots, looting, and the appointment of a Supreme Court judge are just a few of the many things that have caused division and unrest.

For many Christians, we stand afar off and look to our leadership for answers, comfort, confidence, and hope. Just like the children of Israel who were afraid after the divine revelation of the law accompanied with lightning, thunder, fire, smoke, and an earthquake, we are looking for stability in a time of shaking and sifting. What did they see? They saw Moses entering into that darkness, unafraid and with confidence.

Why? Because he knew that God was there! Yes, there is no darkness in God, but we can find God in dark times and in dark places. Just look at the dark periods of church history and you will see that God was working behind the scenes. Also, just look at the darkest moments of your life and see how God was there. Looking back on those times, maybe in those moments you couldn't see him, but you knew he was present.

Two examples:

First, David said in Psalms 23:4, "Yea, though I walk in the valley of the shadow of death thou art with me." How did David know that God was with him? Could he see him? Maybe or maybe not. But he did hear the shepherd's voice.

Second, when Elijah was in the cave, a dark place in the darkest moment of his life, he didn't find God in the earthquake, wind, or fire. But he knew God was there. How? He heard God's still small voice.

What confidence we have in knowing that whatever lies ahead of us, the fact is that our good shepherd goes before us. And if we listen to his voice, he will guide us through it!

Is It Worth It?

(Matthew 16:24–26)

"Is it worth it?"
the devil may ask,
when the cross gets heavy,
when the darts are assailing,
when the arms grow heavy from holding the shield
or wielding the sword.

"Is it worth it?"
some people may ask,
when you have been kind,
faithful,
loyal
because you have done unto others as doing unto
the Lord.

"Is it worth it?"
others may ask,
when you have lost more than you have gained,
when you have been good and
reaped nothing but bad,
when you have given all
and received nothing back.

"Is it worth it?"
Job's wife may ask,
when everything has been lost:

children,
servant,
possessions,
and the respect of closest friends.

"Is it worth it?"
the foolish may ask,
when they don't see
or believe in him,
who you see and love,
in whom you delight
and take pleasure in.

"Is it worth it?"
when I ask,
if he is there
because I feel so empty,
so cold,
wandering,
lost in despair.

"Is it worth it?"
when Jesus asks me,
to take up the cross,
deny myself,
and follow him,
knowing the way is long
and the cross heavy to bear.

"Is it worth it?"
I ask Job,
when he has been perfect,
upright, respectful,
and hating evil.
"Yes," Job says, "it's worth it
because that which is lost, God is able to restore."

"Is it worth it?"
I ask Jesus,
When he calls me to follow
to places unknown,
to do tasks that are hard,
to give my life.
He answers, "Yes." Because his life will be manifested in me.

"Is it worth it?"
you may ask,
when I am doubtful,
fearful,
afraid,
tired,
and weary.

"Yes, it is worth it!"
I say unto you,
and many times over.
For we are just pilgrims in a fallen world,
following Jesus to a place not unknown.
And when we get there, the words of delight we
will hear,
"Well done, thy good and faithful servant.
Enter in the joy of the Lord!"

It's Going to Be All Right
(Isaiah 41:10)

Do you feel turbulent within?
Has your soul been wounded?
Have your expectations not been met?
Do you feel the tension and stress mounting up
more and more?
Have you been tested beyond your strength?

Do not fear, child of God. It's going to be all
right!
Let God speak to you today through this poem.

As the storm was raging
All throughout the night,
I kept hearing the words from my father saying,
"My child, it's going to be all right!"

As I was lying wounded
And he was wrapping the bandage tight,
I kept hearing the words from my father saying,
"My child, it's going to be all right!"

As my expectations
And hopes didn't seem bright,
I kept hearing the words of my father saying,
"My child, it's going to be all right!"

As the tensions kept building
And my confidence turned to fright,
I kept hearing the words of my father saying,
"My child, it's going to be all right!"

When tested beyond all my strength
And I felt I lost my might,
I kept hearing the words of my father saying,
"My child, it's going to be all right!"

As I feel the stress keep building,
The burden is no longer light.
I kept hearing the words of my father saying,
"My child, it's going to be all right!"

So today in our country,
Where day has turned into night,

Don't be fearful, child of God.
For I still hear my father saying,
"My child it's going to be all right!"

It's Not Going to Be Easy
(John 16:33 and Revelation 2:7, 11, 17, 26, 3:5, 12, and 21)

"If it was easy, anybody could do it!" That's what I would hear my dad say a lot when I was growing up. What he was saying was that some things in life will be hard, and not everyone will be able to endure them.

Our heavenly Father tells us the same thing. That life, especially the Christian life, is one that will be difficult yet, with all its difficulties, can be one of joy, which Nehemiah said "would be our strength." Fortunately, we as Christians in America have had it rather easy since the founding of this great nation. In fact, this nation was founded on religious liberty, which offered the opportunity for one to practice their religion without threat or retaliation.

But now, we see that there are threats on the horizon as our constitution is being challenged and in danger of being reinterpreted. There is such a polarization in our political and religious circles now that any chances of coming together in compromise are very low. This scenario sets us up for strife and conflict which, if one side gains the advantage, can persecute the other.

There are already threats against Christianity in America for its identification with conservative values both religiously and politically. If these opponents to the church gain sway, then as already been said by many of its leaders they will seek retaliation on all those who are affiliated with it. The pandemic has also gotten us out of our routines and has forced us into a different way of worship and daily living.

In others words, we are confronted with challenges now that we have never experienced, and life is not as easy or as simple as it once was. If we continue down this spiral of denouncing God, then the challenges will mount more and more. Our Christian heritage may become a thing of the past, and how that shapes the future will determine our willingness to fight the good fight of faith.

"He that overcomes" is what Jesus said to each of his churches in Revelation. So what are the obstacles? Indifference or apathy (Ephesus), tribulation (Smyrna), Satan (Pergamos), false teachers (Thyatira), spiritual deadness (Sardis), temptation or testing (Philadelphia), and worldliness or self-sufficiency (Laodicea).

These things are not easy to overcome but can be overcome through Christ. "We can do all things through Christ which strengthens us!" What strength does he provide? His strength. He reminded his disciples on the night before he died that "in this world you shall have tribulation, but be of good cheer, for I have overcome the world."

Not everyone is going to make it, but they that are in Christ and rely upon his grace daily can overcome because he has already overcome.

No, it's not going to be easy, but it can be and has been done!

Jesus Ran and Hid?
(John 8:59)

Jesus, after claiming that he was God, ran away and hid when the religious leaders sought to stone him. Why? Because his time has not yet come to be seized upon. I would imagine that many Christians in today's world would have criticized Jesus for fleeing instead of staying and confronting his enemies. We would hear words, like "coward," "faithless," "indifferent," etc. The reality of it all is that Jesus was discerning. He knew what to do, how to do it, and when to do it. This is really what discernment is at its core.

Solomon had the same kind of discernment. In Ecclesiastes chapter 3, he said, "There is a time and season for everything under the sun." He goes through a whole list of things to prove that there is a right time to do or not to do certain things.

Jesus knew his purpose, and that purpose was to lay down his life for sinners. This could not just be done at any time or in any way but had to be done in God's time and way. When the time came to for him to die, he would do it and, as the writer of Hebrews said, do it with joy.

My point is this. In this pandemic world we live in, we have to accept the fact that there are times when we will have to do the opposite of what we normally think or are accustomed to. As Solomon said, "There is a time to embrace and a time from embracing" (Ecclesiastes 3:5). Right now is one of those times when we need to cease from embracing.

If Jesus had not discerned their threats, then he would have died before his time, and our salvation would have been in peril. But he did what was right in fleeing the crowd to preserve his life and ministry. Jesus, while speaking about the signs that would occur before the fall of Jerusalem, said, "When you see the armies gather around Jerusalem then flee to the mountains" (Luke 21:20–21). What he is saying is when you discern a threatening situation, run for cover.

This pandemic, much like the enemies of Jesus and Israel, will kill people who are not discerning of its serious potential. I have heard pastors nationally and locally say that there is nothing to it, only to contract it, putting themselves in danger as well as others. We should never downplay the seriousness of something that has been proven to be deadly. The sacrifices that have been made by wise and discerning churches have proven that worship can be done in different ways and settings.

So when Jesus avoided a dangerous situation because of his wisdom, it didn't make him less faithful, neither does it make churches less faithful if they err on the side of caution. Jesus's time came when he did embrace the will of his Father and died on the cross. Our time will come again when we will be able to embrace by worshipping and fellowshipping as we once did, all because of his death on the cross. It's important that, at that time, we lose no one in the process due to our pride or lack of wisdom.

Joy in the Unseen
(1 Peter 1:8)

The Christmas season has always been my favorite time of year. I start celebrating early, generally beginning November 1 by listening to Christmas carols and hymns, watching Christmas movies, and, of course, reading *A Christmas Carol* by Charles Dickens. But over the last few years since my daughter has moved away, Christmastime is an even more joyous occasion because I know she is going to be home for several days, and we get to make up for lost time in between visits. It is an inexpressible joy that you can't explain; you just feel it.

This is the type of joy Peter is writing about. He says that it is "joy unspeakable and full of glory." In other words, it is a joy beyond words and so indescribable that he can only refer to it as "glorious." What fascinates me is that he is describing a love for one who says that his readers cannot see. Peter saw him, walked with him, ate with him, laughed with him, and cried with him. He was there when Jesus worked miracles, when he was taken captive, and after his resurrection. There was no doubt there were many joyous occasions that he shared with Jesus in those thirty-three years.

Peter has the best of both worlds. Not only did he walk with Christ but, as the Bible teaches, Christ at this time of writing was walking in him. This was even more joyous because he knew that wherever he went and whatever he went through, Christ was with him. There were times while Jesus was in the flesh that he would send Peter and the disciples to do certain tasks of which he stayed behind. But to experience the joy of Christ within him was far beyond anything he could describe.

The depth of love that Peter and we ourselves who know Christ have is one that unites us in a way that is much deeper than we could ever imagine. It is a love that produces a joy that resides in the depth of our soul and one that can only be there by the presence of him who brought joy to the world. It is not something that is seen, but it is felt, and nothing can separate us from that love because it abides within us and goes with us even to the far reaches of the world.

How can we love someone we can't see? It is simple! Just as I love my daughter in whom I don't get to see every day like I used to, I know that she is alive, doing well, and accomplishing God's purpose in her life. I know that there is a coming day when she will come home this Christmas season, and I will meet her at the door and give her a big hug. What a joyous time!

I also know that although I can't see Christ, he is alive and serving out God the Father's purpose in the world and in my life, and there is a coming time when he too will come to us and take us to his home, a home he has prepared for us. What a joyous time that will be, even more joyous because then we will see him! "Oh, what manner of love the father has bestowed upon us that we should be called the children of God!" (1 John 3:1).

Joy Restored
(Psalms 51:12)

According to Nehemiah 8:10, "Joy is the strength of the believer." To have it taken away will produce a weakness that will open up oneself to many struggles and unfortunately failures.

Somewhere along the line, David lost his joy in God, and it led to one of the darkest moments of his life. The thing that we need to remember the most is that this happened to a "man after God's own heart." No one in the Scripture outside of our Lord Jesus Christ had a heart for God like David.

It was David's sin that took away his joy, and in this prayer, he asks God to restore unto him his joy of salvation. The joy of being saved is the heart of the Christmas message, and when we have nothing else to rejoice in, we can at least rejoice in the fact that God forgives sin and sinners. Even the most wicked of sins and sinners!

That is why the message from the angels was referred to as "glad tidings of great joy." Even Jesus's own name means "he will save his people from their sins" (Matthew 1:21). Sin brings about a weight or burden that is ultimately difficult to bear. Many people carry the weight and guilt of their sins with them, never able to get over the things that they have done in their past, taking the life of joy and contentment out of them. But the good news is that through confession and repentance of sin and receiving the greatest gift ever given to mankind, that mourning for sin can be replaced by the oil of joy (Isaiah 61:3).

Though sin can take away joy in our lives, it is not the only thing that can. Sickness, suffering, and situations can bring about sadness and cause us to lose focus on what brings us true joy. Jesus told his disciples that in this world there would be much tribulation, heartache, and pain. But he promised them if they would remember that he loves them and if they love one another, their joy would be full.

Peter said in 1 Peter 4:8, "Love covers the multitude of sin." Through God's love, which is demonstrated in Christ, we can rejoice in the Lord and his great work of salvation. But Peter also said that fiery trials would also come along with suffering, but by loving him in whom you can't see, you can still rejoice with joy unspeakable and full of glory (1 Peter 1:8)!

So today, if for whatever reason you have lost your joy, remember it can be restored if you just ask God to restore it.

Kindness
(Romans 12:10)

After having our way of life disrupted now for several months, we are starting to see the effects of what I call the pandemic effect. Many good things have come out of this, but unfortunately, we can see the worst come out as well. Riots, looting, increase in crime, depression, and suicide are to name a few. But one thing I have noticed more than anything is the lack of patience which leads to unkindness. One of the attributes of growing up in the South was its kindness, people being friendly, and, as the old saying goes, "They treat you like family." That's not just a Southern thing. It is a biblical thing!

That is exactly what Paul meant when he said, "Be kindly affectionate towards one another." In other words, love one another like family. That's why we call one another "brother" or "sister" in the Christian community. We are adopted into the family of God by the blood of our elder brother, Jesus Christ. So we are more than a building or organization; we are a community of believers that make up the family of God.

But not only are we to be kind toward one another, the Bible teaches us to be kind to those outside of our family as well. Kindness is one of the Fruits of the Spirit, and it is not based on whether one is kind with us; we are to be kind to them because that's what the Holy

Spirit would do. He is a gentleman. And he wants to bring out those gentleman qualities in you and me as believers.

I was taught growing up that kindness doesn't cost you a thing. You lose nothing by showing forth kindness. In fact, you gain when you show kindness. You may make a new friend or make someone's day. You might be kind to someone who has given up on all hope of goodness in society. Maybe somebody has been mistreated or abused, and an act of kindness may be the very thing that turns their day around.

1 Corinthians 13:4 says, "Love is kind." The affectionate love that Paul speaks of in our text is a brotherly love. So let's seek to be kind to someone today. Even to those who are outside of the faith. Who knows, through our kindness, we may lead someone to Christ—and gain a new family member!

Labor Day
(Hebrews 4:11 and Matthew 11:28–30)

Labor Day is celebrated on the first Monday of September. It is a day set aside where we celebrate the social and economic achievements of the American worker. It was meant to be celebrated by resting from any physical labor on that day, and for many, it is a paid holiday.

We, as Christians, also have a day when we celebrate the rest from the labors that have come from observing the law. The Ten Commandments give us the revelation of God's moral law. God is holy and demands holiness from mankind, but it didn't take long for one to see how impossible a task it was to keep it.

Therefore, being lawbreakers, we needed a means of cleansing and justification in order to be in right standing with God. So he gave us the priesthood and sacrifices, which demand time, energy, effort, and precision. Above all these, it demanded the death of a sacrificial lamb. After hundreds of years of blood, sweat, and tears, we come to the end of the Old Testament and the prophet Malachi. And it has become just a heartless task, and man is lost, in need of a savior.

This was why Paul referred to Christ's coming in the "fullness of time" (Galatians 4:4). What man needed in order to be saved was not another half-hearted, effortless priest offering up a dead sacrifice but a living sacrifice. Not just a sacrifice but also a devoted priest. What man needed and what God provided was the "Lamb of God which takes away the sins of the world." Jesus paid it all!

In Jesus's life, death, and resurrection, we see that he took upon himself the labors that were necessary for the redemption of mankind. He carried the cross. His sweat was as great drops of blood. The anguish from the pain of being beaten and the torments of the mind were the labors he took upon himself on that one day he died upon the cross for our sins. Because of this, the Hebrew writer encourages us to "enter into his rest." This rest is unlike our celebrated Labor Day rest. That is just a one-day observance. The rest we have in Christ's labors is a one-time sacrifice, for all time, by which we celebrate a life of rest.

Today, there is so much labor and civil unrest in our streets, which is the evident token of our country's need for the gospel and revival. No political theory or politician can bring this about, only Jesus Christ!

Read Matthew 11:28–30 and let us celebrate the Christian life, not in laboring to earn God's favor but celebrating the great work of the cross!

Lawlessness and Endurance
(Matthew 24:11–14)

I was looking at a video of a police officer in Wisconsin who was hit by a brick that someone from a group of protesters threw at him. The first thing that came to my mind were the words of Jesus in Matthew 24:12: "Iniquity shall abound and the love of many shall wax cold."

I don't know how you may have reacted when you saw this. There are many different appropriate reactions: anger, sadness, pity for the officer, desire for justice, and many other emotions. The strongest reaction for me is that we have always believed, as Christians, that this day was coming. Jesus said it would. There have been times when we felt that we were *at* this moment. But now, we are *in* this moment. It has arrived, and we have been caught off guard.

IN TIMES LIKE THESE

"Iniquity" is just another word for lawlessness, and it is most definitely abounding in our world today. These attacks have predominately been on businesses, government buildings, statutes, and unfortunately law enforcement. But what will happen when they run out of these things? Will it be homes or churches? Will it remain in the city, or will it spread to the suburbs or even the rural areas? The point is that once iniquity has been let loose, there is no stopping it.

I think it's time we stop living in our fairy-tale world and sober up to the reality that we are living in very dangerous times, and we are not far away, as Christians, from being a primary target in this growing evil.

Jesus said in verse 13, "He that shall endure unto the end, the same shall be saved." We need to be men and women of prayer and arm ourselves with the whole armor of God found in Ephesians 6:10–18. We must fight the good fight of faith laying hold of eternal life. But most of all, we need to do as Jude said. We need to "earnestly contend for the faith."

Jesus overcame evil by his death on the cross, and today the only weapon against the increasing evil in our world is the preaching of the cross.

So here is our twofold challenge: let's endure it through patience, focus, and prayer and let's keep living and proclaiming the gospel. It is still the power of God unto salvation!

Leaning and Upright
(Proverbs 3:5–6)

G K Chesterton said in his book *Orthodoxy*, "There are an infinity of angles at which one falls, only one at which he stands." In other words, having a thorough understanding of God and of man, the human race has the tendency to lean or bend toward sin and depravity. And it is very easy. Solomon talks about leaning here in our text, and the easiest way to lean is *to lean to our own understanding*. We think that we know best, and even when we pray, we find ourselves asking God not only to answer on our behalf but also try to tell him how to do it. When things don't go our way, we become disappointed, discouraged, and even angry, which can lead to stumbling and falling.

God demands uprightness, and the only way that we can truly be upright is to "lean not to our own understanding but in all of our ways acknowledge him and he will direct our paths."

Solomon, in the Song of Solomon, asked a question in the last chapter: "Who is this coming up out of the wilderness leaning on her beloved?" (Song of Solomon 8:5). The answer is those who trust in the Lord Jesus Christ. The only way we can walk upright is by leaning upon Jesus.

So the lesson is that if we lean to our own understanding, we will eventually fall. But if we lean on Jesus, not only will we not fall (Jude 24) but we will also meet God's demand of being upright because it is by trusting in Christ that we stand.

Think of the hymn "Leaning on the Everlasting Arms" today and allow God to "order your steps by his word" so that "iniquity will not have dominion over you" (Psalms 119:133).

Lessons from an Honest Criminal
(Psalms 139:23–24 and 1 John 3:18–21 and 4:17–18)

Victor Hugo, in *Les Misérables*, writes in the chapter titled "The Interior of Despair" of Jean Valjean that "he constituted himself the tribunal. He began putting himself on trial." I love this chapter in the book because even though Valjean is a criminal, at least he is an honest criminal. He was sent to prison for stealing a loaf of bread to feed his sister's children. Not a horrible crime but, nevertheless, a crime. After his tribunal, he acknowledges his guilt.

In this, I think there are a few great lessons that we Christians can learn.

First, I admire his honesty. He thought upon his sin and acknowledged that he was guilty and deserved punishment. The wonderful truth of the gospel is that, yes, we are guilty sinners before God, but it was Jesus that took the punishment. It was a fair punishment and one that Christ didn't deserve, yet because of his love for us, he endured the cross and despised the shame.

Second, it teaches us the importance of self-examination. The psalmist asked God to "search him." The best way that we can know if we have any grieving sin before God is to ask him to evaluate us daily and "see if there be any wicked way within us and lead us into the way everlasting."

Lastly, how good would it be for us to judge ourselves? John, in our Scripture text, says, "If our heart condemns us, God is greater than our hearts. If our hearts don't condemn us, then we have confidence." In the Sermon on the Mount, Jesus taught his disciples that we are to "make peace with our adversary before we go to the judge" (Matthew 5:25). In other words, we do not want to wait until judgment day to confess our sins and try to make peace with God.

The lesson is this. If we judge ourselves by the Bible and the standard of Jesus Christ, then when we stand before him, we can have a good conscience with no fear. Perfect love casts out fear, and one great attribute of a healthy relationship is honesty.

Ask God to search you today and be ready to receive with humility what he finds that you may have neglected to acknowledge.

Let Go and Let God
(Acts 10:1–20)

In reading this devotion, I would like for you to put yourself in Peter's shoes.

First of all, he is a Jew. Growing up as a Jew, he was taught and then practiced not to eat any forbidden food that was outlined in Leviticus 11. Christ, in this vision, has asked him to eat the unclean animals in the unfolding sheet, declaring that what he (Christ) has cleansed, do not call it common.

Second, as a Jew, he has learned from the vision the spiritual meaning of sharing the gospel with a non-Jewish person, a Gentile. Not only is this person a Gentile but also a Roman centurion. He was a military leader of an army that had oppressed the Jewish people for nearly one hundred years.

So here is the dilemma. Peter is being asked by God to forget his Jewish orthodox view of the law and rid himself of his prejudices and hatred toward his enemies. What would you do? There is no doubt that there would be challenges in overcoming this real struggle that, along with Peter, all of us have in one way or the other.

These two things are just a few of many things that stifle the furthering of the gospel. Just think if Peter had said no. What would have happened if he had held on to those beliefs or feelings? The gospel would have never reached Cornelius, and he being a sincere seeker of who the true God is would have died lost, not knowing the Savior of the world, Jesus Christ.

The challenge for us today is the same as it was for Peter. Our culture has changed so much in so little time that the generation gap has grown wider. There is such a difference in thinking between a grandparent and a grandchild that there seems to be no common ground between them. The answer is that we are going to have to get away from the fact that a person looks a certain way or doesn't have the same ideas about things as we do.

We need to trust God that when we share and live out our faith, he through the Holy Spirit will bring about the change of heart that will lead to a change of mind in the life of a lost person. Remember, God looks at the heart of that person. He is like an artist or sculptor. He sees what they can become. He sees their potential. He has chosen us to be the proclaimers.

When Peter agreed to go, he arrived at the house of Cornelius and told him about Jesus. As this was happening, the Holy Spirit fell and saved the life of this Roman soldier. It was the gospel that broke down the barriers and enlarged the kingdom of God. In times like these where we see barriers in our divided cities and cultures, we need to remember that the gospel is still the power of God unto salvation.

So here is the lesson. We take the message; God makes the person!

Let the Redeemed of the Lord Say So
(Psalms 107:2)

Tomorrow is Election Day. It is the day that we go and choose our federal, state, and local leaders. We are very fortunate to live in a country where this is not only a privilege but a God-given right. The freedom to choose is what makes us human and separates us from the rest of the created order. With that choice, we have been given two things: a voice and a vote.

We, as God's people, do have a message. It is a message of his redeeming love for mankind, and it is communicated through preaching and witnessing. It started with a "voice crying in the wilderness" (Mark 1:1–5), which was John the Baptist, and it continues today in and through the church to a lost and dying world. Isaiah encourages the people to "cry loud and lift up their voice and show the people their transgressions and the house of Israel their sins" (Isaiah 58:1). Many people use their voice in singing, acting, and teaching to glorify God and communicate the message of the cross.

The other way we communicate the message is by voting. In every election year, people have the opportunity to choose their leaders by going to the polls and casting forth their vote for the candidate that represents their ideas. The church can allow its voice to be heard by choosing those candidates that they feel represent biblical values, values that influence culture in the way of life demonstrated by Jesus and his followers. To vote for anything contrary to these principles is not being faithful or loyal to our Lord, and to do so means to sow ideas that will cause our culture to reap decay and destruction.

I want to encourage everyone to vote if you haven't already. Every vote does count. Two separate and distinct visions have been laid out before the American people in this election. One recognizes God, life, and freedom. The other is secular, immoral, and fueled by rage and hate. I just pray that Christians will put aside their politics, their party affiliation, and loyalties to family traditions and vote for that which is blessing and not a curse—life and not death (Deuteronomy 30:19). This is where it has come to in our country today, and the choices we make tomorrow will determine where we are going in the future.

Let the redeemed of the Lord say so and let them be heard!

Look of Love
(1 John 3:1–3)

One day, we are all going to see the face of Jesus Christ!

As Christians, we have always tried to imagine what he looks like in the flesh. Medieval artists have tried to paint him, and many others have tried to sculpt him. But obviously these have not done justice and most likely are not anywhere near to his real image.

Yes, we will see him someday!

John saw him on the island of Patmos. After seeing his hair white as wool, his eyes of fire, his feet like brass, and clothed to the foot, John fell at his feet as a dead man. Will that be our response? Will we kneel, bow, faint? The Scripture gives us each of the potential responses.

I am not as much concerned about how he looks as much as how will he look at me? I think the answer to that question is not as hard as we think. I think that he will look at us the way we have looked at him.

If we have looked at him in love, then he will, in turn, look at us in love. If we have looked at him in delight, he will delight in us. If we have looked upon him on the cross in pity, he will look with pity toward us. But not only have we had to look at him, we also have to look to him. If we have looked to him for grace, he will be graceful. If we have looked to him for mercy, then he will be merciful. If we have looked to him for blessing, then he will shine the light of his countenance upon us in delight.

No, we don't know what he looks like, but we will never really know what we look like until we see him. When we look at ourselves in a mirror, we only get a surface look. When we see him, then we will see our true selves as he sees us now.

Our desire is to try our very best to be like him in this life. If we do, then when we see him, he will not look like a complete stranger to us. If this is our desire, then "when we see him, we shall be like him, for we shall see him as he is."

John says if we have this hope, let us purify ourselves. If we do this, then I believe that the look we will see first will be the look of love!

Moral Values
(Exodus 20:1–17 and Matthew 22:35–40)

The word "morality" today has been replaced by the word "values." Morality identifies with religion while values identify with secularism. Morality comes across as judgmental while values are less intimidating and more acceptable. Friedrich Nietzsche, who was antagonistic toward religion, especially Christianity, was the first to replace the word "morality" with "values." His writings still haunt us today as we see the downward spiral of morals and the valuing of the immoral lifestyle.

But I am confused with this upholding of values without morality. For something to be valuable, it must have worth. For something to have worth, it must be cherished. For something to be cherished, there must be love. And guess what? Love is a moral!

Some enemies of Christianity use the argument that if God is love, then why is there so much evil and hatred in the world? The answer is in order to experience true love, then one must love freely and willingly. That's why we have free will as humans. But where there is free will and choice, then humans, being imperfect, make bad choices, which bring about pain and suffering.

But do not values have the same outworking? Communism, which is atheistic in its philosophy, values other people's property, wealth, and land, which led to the death of over one million people in the twentieth century. This was based on a Marxist belief that there should be no classes in society and all should be equal. These same "values" are being promoted by the Liberal Left in our country today, and we see the same outworking of racial divide, rioting, looting, bloodshed, and death. I guess in the "values" code, there isn't any "thou shout not steal, kill, or covet"!

We cannot separate values from morality because they both have in common the moral of love. Have we, as Christians, displayed

95

the godly love as we should have in times past? No! But it's not God's fault; it is ours. It is probably because we have not appreciated God's love for us and, in doing so, depreciated it. But when we value God's unconditional love for us, then we will love him with all our heart, soul, mind, and strength. From that, the outworking of Christian love will follow as we value and love ourselves!

New Year, New Fear
(Proverbs 1:7)

As we embark upon a new year, it is the time for new resolutions. We all, with good intentions, want to be more spiritual, thinner, healthier, financially sound, and just a better person all around. There is nothing wrong with all these, except one thing—we never keep them! Some set their goals too high and are never able to realistically achieve them. Some look at the big picture and never take it day by day. While others come to find out that they really don't want to change. Whatever the reason, what was made as a resolution lacked commitment.

Our Scripture tells us that what we really need to have for successful living is a good wholesome fear of God. It is the fear of God that produces for us the knowledge and wisdom for daily living. The Bible's definition of "fear" is not the same as most people today interpret it. "Fear" today is defined as "afraid," "terror," or "intimidation." But this is not biblical fear. To have a fear of God means to reverence him, to respect him, and to honor and not offend him. When we see and serve God in this fashion, it is then that we become wise and knowledgeable of his ways and his will for our life.

God's will, revealed to us in the person of Jesus and the Bible, teaches us how to live our lives daily for him. It teaches us about salvation and how to live spiritual lives that are empowered by the Holy Spirit. It teaches us how to manage our time and money. We learn how to communicate with others and have good healthy relationships with our families, neighbors, and fellow Christians. It even teaches us how to have healthy bodies, minds, and attitudes.

Our lesson is that the best way to start out a new year, being committed to the changes we want to make, is to start with a good and healthy fear of God. When we remember that we are made in the image of God and that we are bought with the price of Jesus's blood, then that is the first step in having a reverence and respect for God, and everything else tends to fall into place.

No Other Gods
(Exodus 20:1–8)

As God formed the nation of Israel and brought them out of Egypt in redemption, he now brings them to Sinai to consecrate them for sanctification. He gives them his laws for governing a nation. Our nation was built on the same foundation, but where are we now in comparison to then?

Andrew Fletcher said, "Let me write the songs of a nation and I don't care who writes its laws." In making this statement, we see that Fletcher had a concept of the reality of music upon a nation, especially younger generations.

Music has had and is still having a profound affect over the generations of young people in our country over the last six decades, starting at Woodstock and making its way through "We Are the World," Lollapalooza, and the grunge movement of the nineties. The generations that are voting today have been influenced more by cultural philosophers than by Francis Scott Key and our national anthem. Even our churches have suffered a paradigm shift in music and theology because of outside influences and social justice icons.

But it's not only music; it is also Hollywood icons and sports stars. They have as much influence on culture today and have no education in political science or the history and philosophy of politics. When did these become the heroes and icons of the American culture scene? I will tell you when. It was when we made gods out of them.

When you look at our younger generations, you don't see Bibles being carried or crosses being worn, but you see jerseys being worn. These stars and athletes have become our idols. Why? Because we have put sports and entertainment in the place of God. Sunday used to be a sacred day that was set aside for the worship of God and rest. It is not sacred anymore because people opt out of church for ball games, entertainment, and recreation, never acknowledging God and his rightful place in their hearts and society. As a result, when our kids go to college, we lose them to the ideas that these icons kneel for during the national anthem.

The mentality of most people is "We will go to church if we don't have anything else to do." Sunday is no longer the Lord's day. It has been set aside for the National Football League, National Association for Stock Car Auto Racing, Major League Baseball, National Basketball Association, and its icons who no longer stand for the national anthem and who raise their fist in defiance to the ideas that framed our country while, at the same time because of our country and its freedoms, they have become millionaires by selling the jerseys Christians are buying.

Even if people are attending church, we have to be finished by a certain hour in order to get home to watch the game or get to the lake, never thinking about the sermon and what God has spoken to his church. Yet we know the score of every game, the stats of every player, and the lyrics of every song. Scripture memorization is a thing of the past. And we wonder why Christians, when confronted about sin and a sinful lifestyle, say, "I didn't know that was in the Bible."

Don't get me wrong. I am all for social justice, but I believe in addressing that issue Jesus's way by which he put it simply, "Do unto others as you would have them do unto you." Liberal sports stars, liberal entertainers, and liberal big government is not the answer. These have somewhat contributed to the problem we are having on our streets today. But also, liberal Christianity and big liberal churches is not the answer either. The answer is the God who inhabits the universe, coming down into his creation in the person of Jesus Christ, ruling and reining in our hearts as Lord and Savior.

May God forgive us and help us because, in times like these, we need to be as faithful to the Lord as we can possibly be by convincing the nation that if we make gods of people who are mortal and will die, then too it will die. God must be first. "Thou shalt not have no other Gods besides me." Whatever you put first in your life is your god. Meditate on what that is and see if it will save you in the end.

I know that this seems deeply radical, but that's why the early Christians had such a profound influence on Rome in their day. They did not allow the pleasures of that corrupt empire to influence them and therefore take the rightful place of Christ in their hearts. God intends for us to enjoy pleasure, recreation, sports, and other things that are a part of life but never intended for these things to take his place or the people that play them. Most of all, he never intended for them to influence our lifestyle or worldviews.

Am I calling for a boycott? I have learned we can boycott, denounce, and renounce everything that is contrary to our Christian beliefs. But if we don't commit ourselves fully to making Christ the Lord of our lives, we will just find ourselves stuck in the middle not having an influence either way. To put God first means to separate from that which is ungodly and to consecrate ourselves to him as Lord of our lives.

Remember, the number 1 song of today was not the number 1 song of yesteryear. Where are the great actors, athletes, and artist of years past? They are in the grave with only a statute or jersey to remember them by. Only one has died and risen from the grave, and that is Jesus. We don't need pictures or statutes of him. We have the living Christ within us!

Putting on a jersey or hat of a favorite team is fine, just as long as we do as Paul said—to "put on the Lord Jesus Christ" first (Romans 13:14).

Not Certain But Expecting
(Revelation 21:1–5)

As we begin the new year 2021, I can't help but think back on January 1, 2020. That day was like any other typical New Year's Day. Christmas was over, and we started settling in on getting back to normal. One year later, we have learned it was everything but normal.

Along with a new year comes new resolutions, new goals, and the hopes of new things. Maybe you're thinking about buying a new car or a new home or starting a new job. At one time, we could look forward to the new year with a sense of confidence and expectation, but now, all that has changed. With a new administration and maybe more restrictions, it is really hard to look ahead and be encouraged or hopeful. The only thing we can do besides looking ahead is to look up!

I believe this is the central theme and focus in the book of Revelation. It starts out with a beautiful vision of the risen and eternal Christ (chapter 1). It moves on to give the conditions of the church, both good and bad (chapters 2 and 3). Then in the midst of much suffering, pain, and death, the Holy Spirit invites John "to come up hither" (4:1). From here on out, God gives us the reality of the evil that the devil and antichrist will unleash on the world and God's people but also the reality of heaven and the triumph of Christ and his church as the "the kingdoms of this world become the kingdoms of our God and his Christ and he will reign forever" (11:15). Once this is done, there will be a new heaven and a new earth (21:4).

We have experienced so much death, sorrow, and pain and have shed many tears. But in the midst of all these events taking place in our world, God is using them to "make all things new" (21:5). "All of these things are working together for good to them who love God and who are the called according to his purposes" (Romans 8:28). It is hard to imagine a world where there is no heartache, suffering, pain, or death. We can't fathom streets that are safe, cities that are without crime, and leaders that are true and just. But this is exactly what God is planning to do and working toward right now on this New Year's Day in 2021.

As we look back and evaluate the things lost, we can honestly say through it all that God has been with us (21:3). And although we may not be as confident in our politicians, political system, economy, and our relationship with the rest of the world, the one thing that we can be confident in is that God is for us as his people and not against us! And we need to remember that the sufferings of this present time are not worthy to be compared to the glory that will be revealed in us (Romans 8:18).

Although we can't go into the new year with confidence and certainty, we can go into it with expectation. Who knows, maybe this time next year, Christ will have come again and gathered us unto himself. Jesus said, "When men's hearts start to fail for things coming upon the earth, then to look up, and lift up your heads for your redemption is drawing near" (Luke 21:26–28). That is the hope of the church, and Paul said it is a "blessed hope" (Titus 2:13).

Our Advent Journey
(Luke 1:26–38 and 2:1–7)

The Christmas story reminds us of the longing and patience we endure in waiting for the Advent of the second coming of Jesus. When we reflect on Mary and her journey from Nazareth to Bethlehem, it reminds us that the road we are on from this present world to heaven is one that is long and arduous.

As Mary and Joseph finally arrived in Bethlehem, they were tired and looking forward to a nice place of rest. To their surprise, there were no rooms left in the inn, and they were cast out into the cold, finding refuge in a dark, dingy stable to bring forth her Son, the Savior of the world. It was through much labor, trial, and tribulation that Mary brought forth her firstborn son. But what joy she had when she heard his first cry. It was the sound of redemption!

We too, like Mary, have been chosen by God to bring forth Jesus into the world by proclaiming the gospel. Unlike Mary, we do not carry Christ in a womb, but we carry him in our hearts. And just like his natural birth, he awaits us to share him with others that he may be birthed into their hearts. Sharing Jesus with others is a simple task, yet one that is most neglected because of the intimidation that comes along with it. Not feeling adequate, confident, or well versed enough is a form of intimidation in itself, much less the growing animosity toward Jesus in our culture that has increased in the last decade.

Mary felt inadequate to be the mother of the Son of God, but nevertheless, she said, "So be it unto me." What lessons can we learn from Mary on the long journey of restlessness that we are experiencing in this Advent season which is accompanied by a pandemic, civil unrest, and uncertainty?

First, we must *receive* Jesus. Just as the Holy Spirit, in the incarnation, overshadowed Mary and placed the seed of Christ in her womb, the work of salvation is done the same way. Men and women receive Jesus through the new birth. Jesus said, "Except you be born again, you cannot enter into the kingdom of God" (John 3:3). Salvation doesn't come through church membership, good works, or the being the child of Christian parents. Jesus must be received by faith through repentance.

Second, we, as Mary, must *carry* Jesus in our hearts. Paul said, "Christ in us is the hope of glory" (Colossians 1:27). We are not to wear Christianity on our sleeve as much as we are to acknowledge the indwelling presence of Christ within us through the person of the Holy Spirit. The journey is long, and we may grow weary and tired along the way. But nevertheless, Christ is within us and strengthens us daily for the journey through his grace.

Lastly, we must *bring forth* Jesus. Just as Jesus was in her womb and Mary brought him forth visibly into the world, we must make Christ known to the world around us today. How is this accomplished? By conforming to his image, living and acting in the same way as he did. Following in his steps and setting forth a pattern of godliness in an ungodly world.

Our journey in this world as we continue toward heaven can be long, painful, and restless. But what a hope we have in knowing that when Christ comes again, he has a place prepared for us, and the joy of heaven awaits us. When that time comes, it will not be a cry but with a shout, a voice, and a trumpet!

Our Blessed Hope
(Titus 2:11–13)

During the Christmas holidays, people spend a lot of time looking. Whether it is looking for that special gift, watching Christmas movies, even just looking forward to when it is all over, the number of hours or days we spend looking would probably surprise us at how much it takes from what little precious time we have.

Advent is a time of looking. But it was intended to be looking for the return of Jesus and not the commercial or material season that it has become. These things have become a distraction and have caused our eyes to be taken off the true meaning of the season. So many people at this time of year don't celebrate it with the joy of receiving the gift of Christ and the expectation of his coming again to set up his everlasting kingdom on earth.

What we should look for is that blessed hope and glorious appearing of Jesus. In this very different Advent season, there is more despair and hopelessness like we have never seen. All of a sudden, the commercial and material things have been taken away or at least reduced in some fashion or other. Even our relationships and gatherings have been altered, leaving many people isolated and lonely. It has created a longing like never before for our complete redemption that we will receive when Christ appears.

Paul said the "grace of God that brings salvation has appeared." This grace was none other than the incarnate Christ who taught us through his life how to live and be ready for when he appears again not in salvation but to judge the living and dead. By "denying ungodliness and worldly lust, we are to live soberly, righteously, and godly in this present world." This type of living prepares our heart for our heavenly home and doesn't weigh us down with the things of this world.

Our focus then should be on the promise of Jesus that he will come again and receive us. This is the only hope for mankind in eternity. It is a hope that will burst into a glorious appearing by our great God and Savior Jesus Christ. That is why Paul called it a "blessed hope"!

Read also Luke 21:26–28.

Out of the Fire
(Daniel 3:27)

There have been many people rescued from fire. Most who come out of it are either burned or suffer from smoking inhalation. With most, there is some lasting scars or lung damage that is a grim reminder of their accident.

But in our text, there are three young men by the name of Shadrach, Meshach, and Abednego who were delivered out of a fiery furnace unharmed, without burns, no smell of smoke, and not one hair singed. What a miracle! It was their faith in God that brought deliverance. They refused to bow to the idol that Nebuchadnezzar had set up for everyone to worship. They knew that God was able, but if he didn't choose to deliver them, they knew that to suffer for him was to reign with him.

It is by faith that Christians overcome the world (1 John 5:4). Faith is the substance of things hoped for and evidence of things not seen. And by it, many have obtained a good report (Hebrews 11:1–2). In chapter 11 of Hebrews, we see that, by faith and through faith, many overcame trials, tribulations, and torments. The writer goes on to speak of their greatness when he said that "the world is not worthy of them." What a triumph of faith!

But I think the main lesson for us is not only did their faith deliver them from the fire but that it was their faith that put them into the fire to begin with. Faith can get us out of trouble, but it also can get us into trouble as well. Their loyalty and devotion to God was demonstrated in the heat of the moment, and the result of it was that their faith in God brought about the king's ability to be able to see the Son of God in the midst of them. When they came out, they were just the same as before, but Nebuchadnezzar would never be the same.

It was through their fiery trial that the king saw Jesus. God's people are being tested in many ways right now. But instead of seeing it as a trial, we need to see it as an opportunity for people to see Jesus with us, among us, and, most of all, within us, sustaining us in the midst of it.

There were three things they possessed that provided a faith that pleased God:

- their courage,
- their conviction,
- and their togetherness.

But the greatness of faith is not that *we are glorified* by our courage, convictions, and togetherness but that *Jesus is glorified* as our savior and the sustainer of our souls in the midst of our fiery trial.

Painted or Stained?
(Ephesians 2:8–10)

These are some of the most beautiful words in the New Testament. Especially verses 8 and 9. To know that God considers us as righteous through faith in him that stems from his never-exhausting grace should bring delight to any who calls upon the name of the Lord. Grace is God's favor toward man, and grace is not man coming to God but God coming to man in the person of Jesus Christ in whom John said was "full of grace and truth" (John 1:14).

In the proclaiming of the gospel, these two verses (8–9) are used right frequently, as one makes an appeal to another to except Christ in salvation. But it just doesn't stop there. We then need to move on to verse 10 and communicate God's work in sanctification. Paul said, "We are his workmanship, created in Christ Jesus for good works." In other words, we are a piece of work, a work in progress.

God wants to make something out of your life. He created you and wants to create in you something beautiful and something that will bring honor and glory to his name. Just as he took six days to make the heavens and earth and all that is therein, the work of sanctification is a slow but steady progress working toward a specific end. That end is conformity to Christ.

It is believed that Jesus was a carpenter. I tend to believe it because he did build the universe, but more than that, he is a bridge builder. He built a bridge to fill the gap between God and man made by sin. And now he is chipping away here and there, shaping and molding like a potter with his clay on the wheel, making us "vessels of honor, sanctified and made for the master's use" (2 Timothy 2:20).

Keeping in mind the image of Jesus as a carpenter, it would be interesting to see some of the pieces that he made. In reality, we see his work every day when we fellowship with believers. But I have often pondered, would Jesus use paint or stain to finish his projects? I believe he would have used stain. Stain soaks through the wood. It gets deep into it. Paint is just on the surface. It can be easily chipped away.

So what type of finish are you? Painted, which is just surface and can be easily removed through conflict or compromise? Or stain, where your relationship with God is one that soaks through and touches your innermost being which can never be taken off?

Salvation is known as "the finished work of Christ," and what a fine finish it is. Let's give him our finest today!

People Who Are Visual
(Act 16:6–10 and Proverbs 29:18)

One of the things I struggled with earlier on when the pandemic hit was what we are going to do and where we are going to go moving forward with our church. What changes will we have to make, and how well will everyone adapt to those changes? It seems that when I got an idea to do one thing, I just couldn't go through with it, and then I would think of another and couldn't do that either. Finally, I just surrendered to the Lord and let him navigate us through this, step by step and week by week.

This is what Paul faced in our text. He wanted to go to Asia, and the Holy Spirit would not let him. Then he wanted to go to Bithynia, and the Spirit would not let him go there either. Finally, Paul saw a vision of a man that needed help in Macedonia, and the way was opened up for him.

I guess the point is that we don't go anywhere until we get a vision of what God wants to do. There is a place of need that he wants us to reach, and we may not know where that place is now. But in time, we will know.

Until then, we need to pray to be men and women of vision in these dark times. Proverbs 29:18 says, "Where there is no vision the people perish." This really means that where there is no word of the Lord, people will spiritually die. Paul, not knowing where to go, kept proclaiming and discipling right where he was in that moment. I think this is the message to us in this moment as well.

So we may not know where we are heading during this pandemic, but we do know what to do. We must be men and women of the Bible and give visual evidence of the reality of the gospel to the world today.

Gypsy Smith said, "There are five Gospels: Matthew, Mark, Luke, John, and the Christian." Most people don't read the first four, so the Christian is the only Bible that many read. I pray you and me will be read well today!

Perception or Truth
(John 18:33–38 and 2 Timothy 3:13)

Today our culture is driven by perception and not by truth. Perception can be a powerful thing, but it isn't always the measure of reality. Just look at a magician and his magic tricks. It is not based on the truth of fixed laws. But through deception and cunning, it appears to be one thing, when—in reality—it is another. The modern news media are the popular magicians of our day.

To listen to these deceivers is to only get what they want you to know or to distort the truth to promote their propaganda. They will pull the rabbit out of a hat and tell you that the hat came out of the rabbit. In other words, they will tell one lie and then have to use another lie to back up the previous one in order to give the perception that what they are saying is true. They will produce roses out of a cane, but the true way of knowing if what they are saying is true is that you have to smell the roses!

That's exactly what we need to do today in our country: "wake up and smell the roses." This quote means to take time out of our busy lives to consider, think, and observe what is going on around us. As Paul was writing to Timothy about "perilous times," he said that "evil men and seducers shall wax worse and worse, deceiving and being deceived." In others words, they will tell so many lies that they will begin to believe their own lies, having no concept of what is the truth anymore.

Sadly, there are many Christians who have bought into this perception and, unless they have a change of heart and mind, will vote for a godless agenda, thinking that they are doing the will of God. God is a God of truth and in no way has changed what he has revealed unto us in the Bible and through his Son Jesus Christ. To deviate from that is to swerve and make shipwreck of the faith and ultimately, in times like these, destroy the greatness of America in the process.

What the Liberals are introducing is a utopia, not a reality. They use isolated events. And through media and social media, they make it appear that we have a big problem with injustice and are wanting to change the whole foundation of what America is. The truth is that there are some injustices, and Jesus said that there will be. But to judge a whole nation and its future on a few injustices is nothing but Liberals using their power of deceit to promote and hopefully accomplish their agenda.

So what is truth? Jesus said, "I am the way, the truth, and the life. No man comes unto the father but by me." He also said, "They who are on the side of truth listen to me." It is important who we listen to today in our chaotic society. Are we going to listen to the media moguls of the day, or are we going to listen to Christ and the gospel?

"He that has an ear to hear, let him hear what the Spirit is saying unto the churches."

Permissible or Possible?
(Psalms 14:1 and Matthew 19:26)

Russian novelist Fyodor Dostoevsky wrote that "if there is no God, then all things are permissible." He wrote this about 160 years ago, and it was not only prophetic concerning Russia but also his prophecy is relevant to us in our day. After building the greatest nation in the history of mankind where freedom and liberty was not just an idea but an outworking, an accomplishment, we are steadily declining as we have forgotten that rock upon which we were built upon. The text says, "The fool has said in his heart there is no God." This could be better translated as "A fool is one who lives like there is no God." This is America's problem, some Christians' problem, and maybe my and your problem.

The gospel is not just meant for the afterlife and eternity. The gospel is for now as well. It is meant to transform from a life of sin and despair to a life of meaning and hope. It is about conforming to Christ and continuing his work in our present world. It is not just meant to be lived with God but for God. Just as Jesus answered Mary and Joseph as they sought for him and found him in the temple, "Know you not that I must be about my Father's business" (Luke 2:49). That is Christian living!

To live one's life as if there is no God produces what we see in our culture today: riots, looting, protests, taking over cities, defunding law enforcement, lawlessness, school shootings, sickness, disease, poverty, breakdown of the family, and confusion among young people about what is life and what it means to be a man or woman. The answer to all these is found in the Bible, the Word of God.

Jesus said a wise man builds on the rock of his sayings while a foolish man builds on the sand of secular and atheistic ideas and philosophies. In difficult times, they that build on the rock of Jesus's words can withstand challenging situations just as our nation has endured through the civil war, world wars, terrorism, and catastrophe. In times like these, we, as one nation under God, always looked to God. And he brought us through. Now, with leaders who don't believe in God—or if they do, they don't follow his Word—I am concerned that wind, rain, and flood of COVID-19, civil unrest, and polarization in our political system may be the storm that destroys this great nation.

I write this not trying to scare but to make aware the dangers of living as there is no God. But it is not a hopeless situation. Things can change. God can turn this around, but we must first turn around. We need to repent! We need to confess where we have lived our lives like there is no God and start living as men and women under his watchful eye. When we turn to God, then he will turn to us and then turn this nation around and get it on track again.

Yes, if there is no God, then all things are permissible. But I like what Jesus said, "With God all things are possible."

Praying and Waiting
(Luke 1:10)

Over the years, I have come to love this account of Luke's gospel. It is the story of Zacharias and his encounter with the angel concerning the conception and birth of John the Baptist, the forerunner of Christ.

As Zacharias was offering incense in the temple, the people outside were waiting and praying. These two should always accompany each other. They were waiting for Zacharias to come out so that they could know that the nation had been interceded for and that God was pleased and appeased.

Zacharias was offering incense a little longer than usual, and the people began to get really nervous. What they didn't know was that the angel was communicating to Zacharias his role in bringing about God's will for the coming messiah and how his son John would be the one to introduce him.

The lesson for us is that we are like the people standing on the outside, waiting and praying for Zacharias to come out. The difference is we are not waiting for a priest like Zacharias; we are waiting for our high priest Jesus Christ to appear. Until that time, we may wonder what God is up to and how the events going on around us are going to shape up in the near future. We, like the people standing outside in anticipation, don't know what is going on in the counsel of God in heaven. But one thing we do know is that God is up to something. And we, with patience, must wait for it.

God said through the prophet Jeremiah that he knows the plans that he has for Israel and that they are good plans (Jeremiah 29:11). God has good plans for us in bad times, and we just need to wait patiently for those plans to be revealed. Until that time comes, we keep praying as Christ our mediator keeps praying and interceding on our behalf. The revelation will come. The plan will unfold. And God's church will once again take the lead and be the people that he called us to be in times like these.

One day, the eternal plan of God will unfold. One day, the Father will say to his Son, "Go and get my people." We don't know when the conversation will take place. But what we do know is when that day comes, there will be people on earth praying, "Even so come, Lord Jesus"! Until then, may the grace of our Lord Jesus Christ be with us all! Amen (Revelation 22:20–21)!

Pure Religion
(James 1:27)

James tells us that pure religion that is undefiled before God is to visit the fatherless and widows and to keep oneself unspotted from the world.

In many ways, I feel that we are "missing the mark" (which is the true definition of the word "sin") by overlooking these two vitally important things, especially in this moment.

This is where Christians and the social reformers can find middle ground to meet. This is also a good opportunity for Christianity to grow and thrive as well. The early church took it upon itself to look after those in whom they knew needed help and support. Somewhere along the line, the government has taken the responsibility upon itself. Could it be that the church has somewhat failed in this? Could it be because of our prejudices or indifference that we have not been effective in showing the passion and compassion of Christ?

Peter said that "Jesus went about doing good, healing all who were oppressed of the devil" (Acts 10:38). To continue in that example, the apostles set aside deacons to serve the widows and those in need so that they could give themselves over to proclaiming the Word. So the early church saw that it was their God-given responsibility to help those in need. James, in his letter, deals with this extensively.

But also, the other aspect of pure religion is keeping oneself unspotted by the world. In other words, we as Christians are in this world but not of it. A Christian lifestyle is one that should be separate from the lifestyles of the world. It was through the purity of life and serving those in need that led many people to become followers of Jesus.

I can't think of any better example than of Mother Teresa. Her ministry and service in Calcutta is one worthy of reading about. We see in her one who was not of this world but in the world and, most importantly, for the world. Her service and purity reflected that of Christ, and that is what the gospel is all about.

Put Your Trust in the Lord
(Psalms 118:1–9)

I think that one of the lessons I have learned in recent days is that man will let you down. Whether it is a parent, teacher, preacher, politician, or political system, many times we put people on a pedestal. And in the meantime, we are setting ourselves up for disappointment. I remember a preacher from years ago who shared this quote in a sermon: "If you look to yourself, you will be disgusted. If you look to others, you will be disappointed, but if you look to Jesus, you will be delighted."

Many times, we have to be reminded that man is man, and he or she will let us down from time to time.

Our country has surely let us down. There are so many concerns about fake ballots, multiple ballots, and uncounted ballots that we really don't know if our election process is safe and reliable. There is also so much chaos and uncertainty right now as we wait on the outcome of the election that not only affect us but the whole world. Why do we wait with eagerness and anticipation? First, we understand the potential outcome of a government that looks to secular ideas to govern our society which is contrary to the will and ways of God. These ideas will only produce death and destruction of which we are getting a taste of now. Second, maybe we have put so much trust in government, money, material things, and the comforts of our freedom that, without these, we feel anxious. Maybe subconsciously we have made idols out of these things and become dependent on them instead of leaning upon the everlasting arms of Christ our savior.

Our psalm tells us that it is better to trust in the Lord than in man or princes. I thank God for our president and his stance on the values that we hold dear. But as we wait, we understand that he may not be our president any longer. It's all in God's hands. One thing we need to remember is that God is not up for election every four years, and he will never be overthrown! Satan has tried that already and was defeated.

There is nothing wrong with putting our confidence in our leaders. That's why we vote for them. But putting our trust in them is different. "Trust" means to lean upon, to cast oneself wholly upon another because that person, like a giant stone, is immovable. There is only one person that meets these criteria—the person of Jesus Christ. He is the one man and one prince who will eventually become King of kings and Lord of lords that will never be overthrown or let us down!

So look at what's going on in Washington, DC, but don't look to it. Look unto Jesus, for he is the author and finisher of our faith. That's one ballot you can count on!

Sacred or Secular
(Colossians 3:1–4)

Most of us may be familiar with the novel by Robert Louis Stevenson, *The Strange Case of Dr Jekyll and Mr Hyde*. It is a story about a man that has a dual personality. At one time, you see Dr. Jekyll with his inviting demeanor entertaining many friends. Then you see the alternate Mr. Hyde with his evil passions isolating himself in a sense to try his best to keep from committing his evil desire and harming others.

He develops a potion to help him try to suppress the evil within, only to find out that the harder he tries, the more difficult the task and the eviler the outworking. Stevenson writes this book to illustrate the struggle between good and evil in the soul of man. It introduces a

Western idea that there is a dualism in man, one good, the other evil. And whichever one wins in the end determines one's eternity.

We can go beyond the aspect of good and evil and call it in modern terms "the sacred and the secular." This is where Christianity has failed in our Western culture over the last seventy years. For some reason, Christians think that there is a difference between their church life and their work, recreation, and social life. So, for example, we have seen many Christians who on Sunday sing "Oh, How I love Jesus," only to crucify him again on Monday by their evil intentions and harming interactions with others. They are not mindful of the presence of Christ in their life and in no way acknowledge him.

Paul said, "For me to live is Christ" and "Crucified with Christ, nevertheless I live, yet not I, but Christ lives in me." In other words, understanding what Paul taught, our life should not be divided into the sacred or secular. It has to be one or the other, not both! When a person truly comes to faith in Christ, he or she is changed. They become a new creature. Their attitude, affections, and passions change toward sin. And now they long after God, knowing that this world is evil and passing away.

In the Eastern culture, religions like Islam, Hinduism, Buddhism teach that there is not a difference between the sacred and secular. Their religion is not a part of their life; it is their life. This is why you see these religions thrive in that part of the world. Jesus intends for the gospel to bring unity to our life, not dissect it. He said, "If any man will follow me, let him deny himself and take up his cross and follow me. For whosoever will save his life shall lose it, but whosoever shall lose his life shall find it." This is very obvious. You can't have it both ways.

God doesn't want us to just use him to find a church to attend, say prayers when we are in trouble, or use his Word as a source of motivating one's self into increasing self-esteem. He never intended Christ just to be a ticket to heaven. No, he wants us in everything we do to do as unto him and for him. He wants us to make decisions based on his will, according to his way and not on our carnal or covetous desires. This is true worship!

Paul said to seek and set our affections on things above. He said that if you have been resurrected with Christ, he now is your life. Jesus said, "A house divided cannot stand. Either you are for me or against me." You must choose one or the other. In this present crisis, there are two polar opposite visions for the future of our country. One sacred, the other secular. One good, the other evil. How we choose will determine whether God will be worshipped or man. We can't have it both ways!

So where have you placed your passions and affections? Are they on things above or beneath? Are they for Christ who is eternal or for the world which is passing away? Is the life you live yours or God's?

Salty Tears
(Psalms 56:8 and Revelation 21:1–4)

There is salt in tears. That is why there is a sting in our eyes when we cry. The salt is designed to keep out bacteria and dust, also keeping our eyes moist in the process. So in our tears, there is pain but also protection.

Our tears come when we suffer some type of pain. Whether it is physical, emotional, or spiritual pain, they are there to help us cope. But at the same time, there is a cleansing that is taking place, ridding us of things that could cause even more physical pain and suffering.

I believe that there is not one tear shed that God doesn't see. In fact, the psalmist said that "God puts our tears in a bottle." Every drop is stored up as a reminder of the pain that we have endured. He knows every heartache, every loss of a loved one, every disappointment, and every failure that produces each drop of tears.

Tears represent sorrow, but I believe they are God's gift to us to help us cope with each loss. For some reason, after shedding many tears, we find comfort, refreshing, encouragement, and hope. After a while, we feel that everything is going to be all right. Why is this? Because tears cleanse us of our doubts, fears, and despair.

Salt preserves. So the salty tears remind us that whatever has been taken away for the moment has not been lost forever when we have hope in Christ. Salt also heals wounds. Tears have a way of bringing healing to the broken in heart.

The Scripture says that one day God will "wipe away all tears from our eyes." There is coming a day when we will have no need of tears because there will be "no more death, neither sorrow, nor crying, neither shall there be no more pain: for the former things are passed away." Right now, family, friends, loved ones, and church family pass away. In this life, we suffer all types of losses, but one day, the people of God will stop passing away because death will be a thing of the past. It's passing is coming, and that will not cause tears of sorrow but shouts of joy!

Search Me
(Psalms 139)

I sit here under his watchful care,
Knowing that he knows every move I make.
I cannot breathe his refreshing air,
Without him knowing every breath I take.

I cannot get up without my disturbing him.
I cannot lie down if he not tuck me in.
I cannot go to any place on a whim,
Without him meeting me therein.

He knows my thoughts, and that humbles me,
Every word I utter before I even speak.
I cannot turn to run or flee.
Everywhere I look, he is there before me.

Should this terror me? Should I be in fear?
After all, he is my maker and my judge.
Should I tremble when I know he is so near?
Will he, when I offend, hold a grudge?

No, I don't think that he seeks to harm.

For, you see, he knew me from the start.
When in my mother's womb, he formed my arm,
My lips, my lungs, and even my heart.

I have been formed, wonderful in fear.
By his tender hands was I made.
When I came forth and did appear,
He my paths had already laid.

I know that he is with me every step that I take.
He is always by my side.
I know that even when I make a mistake,
He reminds me that it was his Son who died.

For my sins did Christ atone,
Knowing all the while what I would turn out to be.
On the cross, he died all alone.
Such knowledge is too wonderful for me!

In most my holiest moments, I tend to have the
worst thoughts,
Like David when praying, "Thou hast search me."
Strife and hatred mixed with love and distraught,
Oh, what a wretched man I can be.

In life, we tend to go from human to divine,
From the Spirit to the flesh.
But regardless of where I am, he tells me, "You
are mine,"
Reminding me that in him I have rest.

"Search me, oh God, and know my heart"
Was David's prayer and plea.
Know my thoughts from the start
And see if there is any wicked way in me!

Shaped and Sharpened
(Proverbs 27:17)

What is it that influences you the most? What is that one thing that shapes and molds your life? What is it that defines you? What do you want to be like twenty years from now? What do you want your purpose in life to be?

We all remember as children saying, "When I grow up, I want to be a…" You fill in the blank. I don't think any of us ever said, "When I grow up, I want to be perfect, moral, or even a Christian." I definitely didn't want to grow up and be a preacher, but I can truly say God has a great sense of humor.

Our Scripture tells us that "iron sharpens iron." Whether we want to admit it or not, there have been people who have had strong influences on our lives. Some for good and unfortunately some for bad. We all have or have had those special people that we call pastor, coach, or mentor that have helped make us the men and women we are. They have helped shape our beliefs and convictions, and we are appreciative of these people. They are the tools that God uses to shape and fashion us.

But the one person that God truly intends to use to make us disciples is none other than Jesus. He became human to not only tell us but show us what it means to be a man and woman. He showed us that a life of obedience can be one of suffering, yet one that is rewarding and ultimately victorious. In one place, he said, "Take my yoke upon me and learn of me." Paul even said that it is God's will that we be "conformed to the image of his [God's] son."

How does he do this? By way of the Bible and the Holy Spirit. The same word and Spirit that he used in making the old creation is the same word and Spirit that he uses in the new creation. When we walk with him daily in prayer and practice his disciplines in our life, like a blacksmith, he is hammering, shaping, and molding us to conform us to his will and make us more like Jesus.

When we allow God to use his tools to shape and sharpen us, then you and I can be a tool in his hand to shape and sharpen others.

Let us walk near to him so we may be sharp. In times like these, we need a good edge more now than ever!

Silence and the Day of the Lord
(Zephaniah 1:1–7)

It is said that "silence is loud." This is not just a mere metaphor but has been proven medically. When the brain doesn't register a certain amount of noise, then it can produce *tinnitus*. Tinnitus is a condition that causes a ringing or buzzing in the ear that can be random or, in some cases, constant. It is very common among people with hearing loss.

We have become accustomed to so much noise in our world today. Even living out in the country like I do, it is still hard not to hear a plane, train, tractor, or even a tractor trailer. Even most people today have on earbuds and are listening to a playlist or book on their phone or tablet. When we do get those rare occasions of being alone, we just feel uncomfortable with not having someone or something to listen to. Especially in difficult times when we want to pour out our complaints or hear words of encouragement, the silence seems to magnify the problem even more as we have nothing to distract us from our situation.

Zephaniah's prescription for enduring the Day of the Lord is "to be silent before God." In difficult times, we always advise God's people to pray and to seek the Lord. This is good advice, but there comes a point in time when what has been done is done, and there is no changing it. The Day of the Lord is coming for Judah and the surrounding nations, and the only thing that God's people can do is sit silently before him and let him have his say.

In the years proceeding Zephaniah's time, wickedness had its day. The priesthood had its opportunities and squandered them, and their day has come to an end. Now it's God's day, and his instruments of chastening are on their way, and God's people must endure it. God said he is going to "sweep the land," meaning that he is going to wipe away all that which has been sinful, rebellious, and idolatrous. He is going to remove everything that defiles, yet this message is not one without hope. He promised that he would preserve his faithful and restore everything that has been lost (3:14–20). In other words, the Day of the Lord, in this case, was a time of purging and starting over.

In our time, secularism seems to be having its day. The church has had its day for many decades, and like the priesthood of Zephaniah's time, we too have squandered good opportunities. This is a time when God is shaking and purging his church. So we need to remember that God will have his day and his say, and in these moments, we have to sit silently and let him speak.

Anyone who has ever sat in on a trial knows that when the judge walks in, there is reverence and silence. He or she has the authority to execute justice and judgment according to the law. Just as in Zephaniah's day, the Day of the Lord had come, and all that the people could do was be silent while he executed his judgment. If there are any words uttered in prayer by his people during a time like this, it should be "Thy will be done!"

Many are saying that our day is a day of darkness, much like the Day of the Lord. Who knows? But if there was a time for us to accept things because we don't have the power to change them is now. It is a good time for us to get used to the silence and let God have his say-so.

My challenge is that whatever is overwhelming you today, you try to silence the voices of doubt, despair, and unbelief. Give no place to the devil and his demonic lies and accusations. Sit still and know that God is God. Listen for his still small voice and fill your mind and heart with his exceeding precious promises.

Sit Quietly and Wait
(Lamentations 3:1–26)

In times like these, we may not only feel afflicted like Jeremiah here in our text. But we may also feel conflicted, vindictive, and, as patriot of our country, neglected. When you feel like you have lost something meaningful to you, it is natural and easy to react this way. Jeremiah, in verses 1–18, feels the anguish, pain, and suffering of a fallen city and its people.

Jeremiah sees the destruction of a city that he spent forty years trying to save. He is known as the weeping prophet, and he wept so much for the sins and unbelief of the people. He was also ignored, ridiculed, beaten, and imprisoned all because he cared.

Now that the city has fallen, he is sitting among the ruins and begins to write the book of Lamentations. It is considered to be a dirge or what we call a funeral song. And it describes the depth of pain, sorrow, and anguish of a man of God and a patriot. Many times, he would look at the city from afar and would just weep of its impending doom if the people would not repent and change their mind toward God. I think that many did repent, but the leaders of the nation were so far gone in their corruption, greed, and godless agenda that the Lord had no choice but to chasten and punish the nation.

Now he sits among the death and destruction, pouring out his heart to God for mercy and hope.

We too are witnessing before our very eyes the collapse of another nation founded by God. I believe that many have turned back to God over these last several months, but like Jerusalem of old, it is our leaders that are bringing about this fall. The same sins of corruption, greed, and godlessness is leading to chaos and confusion. And we don't know who or what to believe anymore. But just as Jeremiah found hope in his despair, we too have hope in ours.

Although Lamentations can be very dark, we have to remember that when light shines into the darkness, the darkness has to flee (John 1:5). That ray of light and hope was found in the:

- mercy of God (verse 22),
- faithfulness of God (verse 23), and
- availability of God (verse 24).

It is after this that Jeremiah could move forward and finish the work that God called him to do. He understood that the best way to do that was to "sit quietly and wait on the salvation of the Lord" (verse 26). Although he preached the promised judgment, he also proclaimed that God would build Jerusalem back up again seventy years later.

It is believed that in the very spot that Jeremiah wrote Lamentations would be the very spot at which Jesus was crucified, buried, and rose again. The death of a nation is one thing, but the death that we face from sin is another. If Jesus could overcome the greatest enemy of mankind which is death, then surely by the mercy, faithfulness, and availability that we have in God, he can carry us through and help revive us as a nation again to be that one nation under God once more! Amen!

So Human, So Divine
(Luke 8:22–25)

I am always so fascinated when I read this account in the gospels. In it we see the uniqueness of Jesus Christ in that he was so human and yet so divine.

Jesus was so human that he was tired and needed sleep. He had been ministering all day and was worn-out. He was so worn-out that when a storm came up, unless they had awakened him, he would have slept through it. Why could he do so? Was it because he was very tired and in a deep sleep? Maybe. But I also believe that Jesus trusted his heavenly Father to such an extent, that when he would pray Psalms 4:8 before lying down, he knew that God would sustain him. It is the same with us in these turbulent times we are living in. When we lie down at night and pray this psalm as well, we too can have that same quiet confidence and trust in God.

Jesus was so divine that when they woke him up, he rebuked the wind and waves and brought calm to their situation. We are not much different from these disciples. We do panic when it seems that everything in life is falling apart. Being pulled here and there, we don't know where to go or what to do. Thank God that, just as Jesus was in the boat with the disciples, he is in our situation as well, and all we have to do is go to him in prayer. Notice that he slept through the storm but was awakened by their cries. In doing so, he brings about a peace, a calmness to our turbulent souls.

Finally, we learn that Jesus is so human that he can identify with our griefs and fears, and yet he is so divine that he can intervene into our situations and bring about the calm and assurance that he will bring us to the other side. This lesson demonstrates his power over the elements for the serving out of his purposes and for the benefit of his people. I just wonder how many times he intervened over a situation that was potentially harmful to us that we don't even realize and, in doing so, protected us from imminent danger.

So it would serve us well each day, not only to thank him for the things we know he does for us but also for the things we don't know he has done.

Jesus is so acquainted with our humanity because he is in us and yet so divine that he goes before us. What confidence we have in him knowing that in this journey we have begun with him, he has not only brought us this far but will bring us to the other side.

Spiders in the King's Palace
(Proverbs 30:28, Psalms 19:12–13, and Romans 6:14)

I can't stand a spider! I know that they are God's creatures, but if I see one in the house, I kill it. The thought of that thing roaming around in my home and ending up in my shoe or my bed drives me insane. The damage that some spiders can cause is severe sickness, tissue damage, and, in some cases, death.

The Scripture says that spiders are found even in the king's palace. There is no doubt that the palace of a king was spotless. It was cleaned on multiple occasions and guarded very heavily. It was made better than any building and would have been well protected from any pest or dangerous animal. Yet the spider could be found in the most beautiful of all mansions.

What is the lesson? Sin is much like the spider. It doesn't matter how holy and how guarded we are; we still possess even the smallest of sins. Even the most godly and devout people we know, if they were honest, would confess that there is within them something to confess. Some struggle, some temptation, some nagging thing that is always crawling around, making itself known. It's like when God

PASTOR ROBBY STEWART

came to Cain and told him that "sin lies at the door and it wants to rule over you, but you are to rule over it."

So what do we do to the creepy, crawling, nagging of sin? We squash it! We stomp on it! We don't let it continue to live and multiply, causing little sins to lead to big sins that we have to contend with. Spiders are small and dangerous, but we are much bigger and have the power to kill them. Sin is the same way. Just as the spider is small enough to grasp with the hand, we can put our sin in the hands of God by acknowledging and confessing it in our life. Paul said, "Sin no longer has power over you because you are not under the law, but grace" (Romans 6:14). "Where sin abounds grace much more abounds" (Romans 5:20).

We, as the temple of God, are a beautiful palace just like the king's palace. But we too, like those spiders, have our creepy, crawly, nagging sins that must be acknowledged, confessed, and turned away from.

Is some nagging sin dominating your life? Then put your foot down and crush that sin through the power of God's grace and Holy Spirit.

Spilt Milk and the Word of God
(James 3:1–18 and Psalms 107:20)

One of my favorite essayists is F. W. Boreham. He wrote an essay titled "Spilt Milk" (from *A Reel of Rainbow*) that got me to thinking about the power of words. This was not what his essay was about, but I took his principal thought and began to think about what James said about the tongue. He gives almost an entire chapter to describe its destructiveness.

I have always believed that social media is one of the many things that have been used to destroy our culture. Don't get me wrong; it has its usefulness when rightly used. But we have to be careful what we say in a post because once it's out there, especially for any length of time, there is no getting it back. This is the power of words. Good or bad, they will not return void; they will prosper for good or bring pain wherever they are sent.

126

There have been things said years ago that still haunt people today. Hateful or abusing words from a parent, family member, or former friends that have shaped or molded a person's life for bad. What's really sad is when Christians do this. The hurt is that much more magnified. So let us choose wisely what we write or say.

James says that the true character of a Christian can be determined by their words. We can dress it up outwardly, but as the old saying goes concerning the heart, "What comes up, comes out." Some make this statement when talking about their honesty or truthfulness, but it must be done as Paul said, "Speaking the truth in love." What we are seeing and hearing today in politics, the media, and on the streets is not love but hate. We, as the church, must be different. James said good and bad language cannot come from the same source. Words of love and hate cannot come from the same heart, just as salt and fresh waters can't come from the same fountain.

The reason why this is important is because words are like spilt milk. Once you spill milk on the ground, you can't get it all back. At least water will soak into the earth and go back to the stream or ocean from where it came. Milk cannot go back to the cow. Once it's gone, it's gone, and it is a waste.

Many lives today have become a waste. Our cities are becoming a waste, and the reason is that we have wasted our words. The words we need to hear are God's Words. Jesus said his words are "Spirit and life." God's Word is prosperous and brings forth the fruit of righteousness.

What will heal our land today? God's Word and the gospel. Psalms 107:20 says, "He sent forth his word and healed them from all of their destruction." Let us proclaim the gospel today so that, at the end of it, we are not crying over the spilt milk of wasted words and lost opportunities!

Spirit Filled and Spirit Flowed
(Ephesians 5:18–19)

As I was sitting and drinking a cup of coffee, there was a lady waiting in line humming the song "Come Thou Fount of Every Blessing." I want you to know the fountain poured forth! What a blessing it is in a world full of strife, affliction, and suffering that the peace of God can override all the noise.

I did not know this lady and have never seen her before. I have sat at this same table many times and have seen many of the same people, but never this lady. I noticed that not only I but others as well were blessed by her song. Was she an angel? She could have been. Was she from out of town? She could be. All I know is she was in the right place at the right time.

We, as Christians, know we are blessed every day, and we look for blessings because we expect them. After all, God promises to bless those who bless him. But even though we know and expect them, God still has a way of catching us off guard, and that is the blessing of blessings!

My point is this. I think it is important for us to do as Paul said, "Be filled with the Spirit." Having the fullness of the Holy Spirit daily in our lives is not only essential for us but for others as well. How do we maintain the fullness? By singing psalms, hymns, and spiritual songs, making melody in our hearts to the Lord.

When we do this, not only will we be doing this to him but we will also be doing it unto to others as well, being a blessing unto them. In these past few months of pandemic and civil unrest, it has left many people discouraged, lonely, afraid, and hopeless. Some people have even questioned whether life is even worth living anymore. Then comes along someone like this lady, who can not only make someone's day but turn around their whole life.

It reminds me of the words of Jesus: "When you have done it unto the least of these, you have done it unto me." This lady, being filled with the Spirit, was a blessing unto all of us and, in turn, was blessing and praising God. It was as if she was using the hymn as a prayer for God to pour out his blessing upon us. And he did!

Through her song, I knew that she was blessed by God. But God very seldom blesses us for our benefit. He blesses us for the benefit of others. This lady's song was my blessing for the day.

So let us "praise God from whom all blessings flow, praise him all creatures here below, praise him above you heavenly hosts, praise Father, Son, and Holy Ghost." Amen!

I believe the floodgates just opened!

Spiritual Prayer
(Jude 20–21)

The only way to combat all that is going on in times like these is through prayer. But not just prayer—spiritual prayer!

Jude's letter talked about perilous times and evil running rampant. Not just evil things but also evil people. He wanted to write about the common salvation, but the Holy Spirit guides him into a different direction, encouraging the saints to "earnestly contend for the faith" (verse 3). After giving a list of the prevailing conditions of his day, he then encourages them "to build up their most holy faith, praying in the Holy Spirit" (verse 20).

I think that the only way we are going to be able to "keep ourselves in the love of God" (verse 21) is to pray fervently and spiritually in these dark times. This takes focus! We have to lay down the news media, social media, and other outlets and hear the good news of the gospel, which comes from prayerful reading of God's Word. As long as we keep taking in the events of the world and not balancing it with hearing from heaven, we are going to be fearful, doubtful, neglectful, and ineffectual in our everyday life.

James said, "The effectual, fervent prayer of a righteous man avails much." Fervent prayer gives us boldness, power, focus, and faith to believe all things and be all things for Christ in times of testing. But not only should we pray in the Spirit, we will also be able to speak in the power of the Holy Spirit, knowing that he will give us the words to say as we defend and share our faith before others.

I want to encourage you to build up your faith through spiritual prayer in a time when foundations are being destroyed. In spiritual prayer, it is the Spirit in you, praying for you and through you! It is through this type of praying that we know "all things will work together for good to them that love God and are the called according to his purpose" (Romans 8:28).

For further encouragement, read Romans 8:26–28.

Still

(Psalms 46:10, Exodus 14:13, and Mark 4:39)

"Be still and know that I am God."
Let all the earth be silent before him.
Bow your head in reverent nod.
Soak in his presence, be filled to the brim.

"Stand still and know that I am God.
You need not weary against your foe.
For it is I who before you trod,
Clearing the way as you go."

"Peace, be still," Jesus said unto the storm
As the disciples rowed in anguish and fear.
And the winds calmed and went back to norm.
The disciples were relieved, their hearts full of cheer.

"Be still before the Lord," David would say.
Wait patiently and calmly for him.
For the evil man will have his day.
Judgment for the wicked will be grim.

I will be still and know that he is God.
I will be silent before him.
I'm humbled. I bow my head and nod.
By his presence, I am overwhelmed.

I will stand still and observed from afar.
I will rest while he wars.
He has won the battle with his scars.
His triumph on the cross is mine and yours.

"Peace, be still" were the words I heard,
When on sin's stormy waves I was tossed.
The calmness that I felt at his spoken word,
I knew I was found and no longer lost.

I will be still and wait patiently for him,
For he will soon come again.
And he will judge the quick and the dead,
But then I will be still, as I hear him say, "Enter in!"

Stirred Up
(Deuteronomy 32:11 and 2 Timothy 1:6)

"As the eagle stirs up her nest!" That's what we need—a good stirring! The eagle is a bird that is found in the Scripture on several occasions. In most of these references, God uses the eagle to illustrate himself and his dealings with Israel. The eagle is the highest soaring bird with the best eyesight. It provides a nest for its offspring that is comfortably padded and nourishes them abundantly until they come of age. At first, they do not want to leave the nest because of the comfort and ease of nourishment. So the mother "stirs up the nest" so that the sharp edges of the twigs poke through and bring pain to the younglings. If this is not successful, then she will toss them out and let them fall, only to come to their rescue before hitting the ground. This stirring up and casting out teaches the young birds two things: to fly and to trust.

Sometimes in our relationship with the Lord, we can get too comfortable and really indifferent. It is okay to be dependent on God because that is what faith is all about. But God has made us to soar. He doesn't want us to become so comfortable in the nest of the four

131

walls of the church but wants us to go out and share our faith. Prior to the pandemic, we were comfortable and spiritually out of shape. But when COVID-19 hit, we were forced out of our comfort zones and had to become creative in our worship. And it worked! The gift of God was stirred up within us (2 Timothy 1:6). Christians were praying more, reading more, sharing more, and talking more about Christ than ever before. In other words, we felt as though we were falling, but God came and swooped us up and carried us through.

But also, we have learned to trust God. We have been put in a place of which we can no longer lean to our own understanding but in all our ways to acknowledge him (Proverbs 3:5–6). We have found out that surely God's ways and thoughts are higher than ours, and though we do not know at times what he may be doing, what we do know is he knows what he is doing.

I am in no way trying to lessen the importance of our assembling together. It is biblical and healthy. But Christian worship and living is done outside of the church (or should I say nest) more than in it. We should soar in the opportunities of Christian witness that God has given us and trust that the words we say will be powerful, influential, and impactful.

I am praying this morning that God will use this devotion to stir up his gift in you!

Surprised by Joy
(Psalms 16:11)

I love to read or hear about people's conversion stories. I'm fascinated that God brings many people to himself from many different walks of life and in many different ways. What all this has in common is that all these different paths lead to one path. And it's that one path that leads to joy.

David said, "You will show me the path of life." God has clearly shown unto the world the way back to him. It was announced by the angels on the Christmas night, lived out by that baby who grew up to be the Savior and displayed before the world his love at the cross. By his triumph over the grave, Jesus clearly illustrates to the watching world that he is indeed "the way, the truth, and the life." The expression of joy just leaps off the page when you read the postresurrection stories and the reactions of those distraught disciples. Their sorrow had been turned into joy.

Jesus is not only the path of life but he is also the way to joy. True joy is found in having a personal relationship with him. This relationship is one that brings pleasure from his abiding presence, and wherever his presence is, there is light. For he is the light of the world. So no matter how dark of a time we may be in, we can still experience the joy of knowing and being with him because we are in him and he is in us.

One of my favorite conversion stories is told by C. S. Lewis. He was raised in a Christian home, but after going off to college and fighting in World War I, he had lost faith and became a devout atheist. After the war, he made friends with some professing Christians, and that began his journey back to God. At first, he became an agnostic, but after investigating the truths of the Bible and following the evidence where it led, he confessed that he was the most reluctant convert to enter into the kingdom. And he came in kicking and screaming. But when he finally gave in, he confessed that he thought he was coming to a religion but soon found out that he came to a person, the person of Jesus Christ! He was so overwhelmed by joy that he wrote an autobiography of his life and journey and titled it *Surprised by Joy.*

The path of Jesus led him to a life of joy. Are you not feeling joyous today? See which paths you have been taking lately that have led to your sadness. Then pray and seek for God's presence in your life today through Jesus who brought joy to the world.

Take Heed to the Message
(Genesis 19:1–26)

On the eve of God's judgment on Sodom and Gomorrah, Lot's message to his sons-in-law was not taken seriously. This had to be very disappointing to Lot. What's even worse is that on the way out of Sodom as they were going to Zoar, Lot's wife didn't take heed to the message of staying focused and of not looking back. The sons-in-law died in Sodom, and Lot's wife was turned into a pillar of salt, all due to their unbelief.

We have the tendency in good times to not take heed to the truths of the gospel. What's even more disturbing is not taking heed to it when obviously its prophecies are coming to pass right before our eyes. I think that in this present crisis, we need to start taking the gospel more seriously than ever before. The time at hand is very critical. And so much hinges on how we, as God's people, take heed to the mission that is set before us to acknowledge the reality of God's impending judgment upon our nation.

Maybe Lot's sons-in-law didn't take him seriously because Lot didn't take it seriously to begin with. We don't realize sometimes just how much nonbelievers observe our life and make judgments based on not what we say but what we do. The angels have to hasten Lot to get him out of there simply because Lot was tempted to procrastinate.

But the Lord was merciful to him. It is evident that with the pandemic, civil unrest, natural disasters, and tension among the nations of the world that something on God's prophetic calendar is going to happen. We should not take these things lightly but seriously.

So let us do as the Hebrew writer said in Hebrews 2:1: "Let us take the more earnest heed to the things that we have heard lest we let them slip." Let us take heed to the sermons that we hear. Let us take heed to the signs we are seeing. Let us take heed to the symptoms of our dying nation as we have turned away from the living God!

In times like these, let us learn from this biblical story and not mock, procrastinate, or look back. Let us hear the words of Christ when he said, "Remember Lot's wife!"

Take Off the Mask
(James 5:16–20 and Romans 15:1)

There have been a lot changes in our daily living during this pandemic, but I think the biggest and most frustrating one has been wearing a mask. I just simply can't get used to it. Sometimes I will forget to put it on, and after wearing it so long, I sometimes forget to take it off. Some say they protect us; some say they protect others, and many say they don't protect at all. Regardless of their usage, it has suddenly become a way of life, and most people don't like it.

But really wearing a mask is not anything new, at least in our spiritual life. Whether one acknowledges it or not, we tend to put on mask from time to time in our spiritual walk, and we do it not to protect others but to protect ourselves. We put on the mask of a fake smile, false joy, and false security. We also tend to put on a fake righteousness, a pretentious love, or false Christian profession so that we appear to be a person we are really not.

This is the great contrast between the early church and the religious Pharisees in the first century. The early Christians were not ashamed to recognize their struggles, weaknesses, and fears. They would gather together and confess their faults, exposing their true selves before one another. This never created division, but it brought a commonality into the Christian community. They found that they were like Elijah "who had like passions" just like themselves.

The Pharisees, on the other hand, were the opposite. They dressed up their religion and pretended to be something they were not. Jesus said that they were "like whited sepulchers, beautiful on the outside, but on the inside full of dead men's bones" (Matthew 23:27). Jesus could see right through their pretension, and he also sees through ours.

Paul said that the strong believers should consider the weak believers (Romans 15:1). Strong believers are not the ones who are sinless, never having their struggles with weakness or temptation, but are those who confess these things before an all-seeing God, praying for his grace and mercy every day. The weak believers are the ones who depend upon their own strength and goodness, judging others for their weaknesses of which they fail to acknowledge in their own lives.

So the only remedy toward having an intimate relationship with God and one another is to take off the mask. We should strive to be honest with God in our weaknesses and patient with our brothers and sisters in Christ with theirs.

The mask over our face may or may not protect us from the virus, but taking off the mask of self-righteousness and hypocrisy will protect us from falling in to deeper sin and causing others to stumble along the way.

The Day of Small Things
(Zechariah 4:10)

We miss so many blessings and opportunities because we expect big things from God. There is nothing wrong with believing God for big things, but he does his biggest work in small ways, and we have to have the faith and discernment to see it.

Zechariah along with Joshua were given the task of rebuilding the temple after the return from Babylonian captivity. It was a big task that was going to be done in small steps. This sounds like a similar situation for us today.

During these days of pandemic, civil unrest, and uncertainty, we must be looking for the little things that God is doing to bring about the big picture. Some of the most beautiful puzzles are made up of many small pieces, and as each piece falls into place, the picture becomes more discerning. We don't know exactly what God is doing or where things are going. But as each piece comes together, we will, as the old hymn says, "understand it better by and by."

Many of God's people in the past saw God moving in the small things. Noah had an olive leaf in a dove's mouth to show him that it was okay to get off the ark. All Elijah needed was a cloud about the size of a man's hand to know that there was going to be an abundance of rain. Moses had just a staff, but it brought about great plagues that led to the deliverance of God's people out of Egypt. Solomon said that we can learn a lot just by watching the ants.

So I want to encourage you to take some time alone with God in prayer and ask him to help you see the little things he is doing in your life during this pandemic and civil unrest that will increase your faith and help you see that he has big plans for you and his church. Let us not despise the day of small things.

If the little foxes can spoil the vine, then surely a small mustard seed of faith can move mountains!

The Eternal Vacation
(Psalms 16:11)

Being on vacation for a week not only gives one time to relax and enjoy the destination but also gives one time to think and put things in perspective. One question that seems to come up is "What truly makes me happy?" For some, it may be a place; for others, it may be material things or money. Some might even say it is a person, like a spouse, sibling, or friend. No doubt, all these may bring pleasure and happiness, but God created us for more than just these above-mentioned things. These are just by-products of the true source of happiness which is God himself.

David said that "in your presence is fullness of joy, at your right hand there are pleasures forever more." He found that only God can bring the contentment and satisfaction that we, as humans, long for. Through five months of this pandemic, we have no doubt been limited in what we can do and what we once enjoyed. We miss our favorite restaurant or going to our normal vacation spot. And some have even lost their businesses or jobs, and yet they have maintained a joy and quiet confidence in the Lord, knowing that he cannot and will not be taken away.

How do we arrive at this point? David said in verse 8, "I have set the Lord always before me; therefore, He is at my right hand." When we order our lives the biblical way, we find that true contentment comes in having a relationship with Jesus Christ. He is symbolized here in the psalm as being the right hand and visible presence of God. Life, careers, recreation, material things, and relationships are only as good and meaningful when we are in a right relationship with God.

Saint Augustine said, "You have made us for yourself and we will not find rest until we find it in you." He was obviously talking about God. Put God first in your life, and all other relationships and pleasures will find their rightful place and meaning.

Vacations are good and restful, but as we all well know, they go by fast. The pleasure, rest, and contentment that we have in Christ will be eternal!

The Example of Love
(John 13:34)

Jesus came to earth not only to tell us of God's love but demonstrate his love as well. Jesus is not only the greatest expression of love; he is also the greatest example of it. "Just as I have loved you, so you love one another."

Our greatest tendency is to forget and take advantage of God's gift of love to us and fail to extend it to others. At the close of the Old Testament, the prophet Malachi opened his prophecy by sharing God's Word to the people with an emphatic statement and indifferent response by the people. God said, "I have loved you." But the people responded by saying, "In what way have you loved us?" Israel had become so indifferent to God's love, and that indifference had extended out toward one another. The result was that it became the lowest spiritual point Israel had experienced since the return from Babylon.

At the end of the first century, John writes the book of Revelation, and the last words to the church of Ephesus were "You have left your first love." Their works were commendable, their doctrine sound, but their love had faded.

Love is usually the first of our emotions to go when we begin our spiritual decline. I believe that's why Jesus talked about love more the week before he died than he did the three and half years leading up to this time. So what kind of love did he love them with?

- unconditional love
- patient love
- protective love
- brotherly love

139

Why is love so important to God and us?

First of all, God is love. John, in his first epistle, conveys this great truth about God.

Second of all, love in action demonstrates the message of the gospel and makes it much more effective.

Finally, love covers a multitude of sins. The most effective way to win a sinner to Christ is to love them the way Christ did, not for what they do but who they are. Jesus died on the cross while we were sinners (Romans 5:8) to show the world that man has value in him. We must remember the vilest sinner is still made in the image and likeness of God and is valuable enough for God to give his Son.

One of the greatest compliments the first-century church received by the unbelieving world was "How those Christians love one another!" This Christmas season, we are faced with challenges like we have never experienced before. But the way we are most effective is by showing the world the love of Jesus, and the best way to do that is to do unto others as he does unto us!

The God Who Shows Mercy
(Romans 9:16 and Titus 3:5)

Paul is writing to the church in Rome about the gospel. It is an in-depth epistle that goes into great detail on the theological and practical components of God's redemptive plan for Israel and the Gentiles. It appears that after the work of the cross and the proclamation of the gospel throughout the known world, God had forgotten about his covenant with Israel. Paul writes to assure the Roman believers that the nation of Israel still has a part in God's plan.

In fact, all of mankind has a part in God's plan. The gospel is for everyone and that whosoever believes upon Jesus will have everlasting life. But that is the key to the gospel. It's about believing, and believing requires faith. So Paul, as he is dealing with Israel in this ninth chapter, reminds the Roman believers, as well as you and me, that salvation is a gift of God. It cannot be earned or inherited.

Paul wrote that "it is not unto him the runs or to him that wills, but God who shows mercy."

"To run" is an athletic term meaning that it is not something acquired by some physical exertion or some moral discipline. "To will" means to seize with the mind or to purpose one's own way to salvation. In other words, it is not an intellectual achievement. So having concluded that it is not to the moralist or gnostic that will earn salvation, it is the one who throws himself or herself upon the mercy of God.

This contrast is given by our Lord in the parable of the Pharisee and the publican (Luke 18:9–14). The Pharisee trusted in his own morality and knowledge of the law. The publican, who was looked down upon in Jewish society for his thievery and loyalty to Rome, was nothing but a standard of measurement for the Pharisee to boast in his self-righteousness. Christ would go on to hear the prayer of the publican who sincerely acknowledged his sins and confessed his need for God's mercy. Mercy is the loving kindness of God toward man. It is God showing pity to miserable sinners.

Anyone who has, is, or will ever be saved has done so because God showed mercy to him or her. We cannot be morally disciplined enough or acquire enough knowledge to pull ourselves up by our own bootstraps and make us righteous enough to stand and give an account unto God. It is "not by works of righteousness which we have done, but according to his mercy he saved us by the washing of regeneration and renewal of the Holy Spirit" (Titus 3:5).

Not running and willing but washing and renewal. This is how we enter into the kingdom of God, and one enters by crying out, "God, be merciful to me, a sinner!"

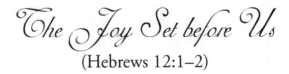

The Joy Set before Us
(Hebrews 12:1–2)

The writer of Hebrews described the cross of Jesus as the "joy set before him." How could so much pain and suffering be approached by so much joy? Jesus looked beyond the suffering and shame and saw the redemption and reconciliation of mankind back to God.

Redemption is what the Christmas story is all about. To redeem something or someone means to buy it back. There was a price to be paid for sin, and that was death. This death for sin is universal to all of mankind, and so every man needs to be redeemed. That's why the message that night was good news to all men. Jesus took it upon himself to be that redeemer, and the only way it could be accomplished was through the cross.

This great work of redemption began with Christ coming to earth through the virgin birth. Not only was his death complete suffering but, even in his birth and life, he endured hardship and affliction, taking upon himself the sins and sickness of mankind. Yet in the midst of it all, he did it with joy. Pain and suffering can either be central in our life or peripheral. G. K. Chesterton said, "To the believer, joy is central and sorrow is peripheral, but to the unbeliever, sorrow is central and joy is peripheral." How a person deals with it is determined by what he or she focuses on.

Jesus focused on the triumph that would come by way of the resurrection. In times like these, we are experiencing suffering and affliction like we have never seen. To many, it has caused fear and despair, but to some, it has created a longing for the triumph that will come when Jesus comes again.

So let us, as we travel toward our heavenly home in this valley of tears, keep looking unto Jesus, the author and finisher of our faith. The good tidings of great joy that came in the darkest hour of the night in that first Advent are the same glad tidings that are still being proclaimed in this dark Advent season. In this present darkness, let us be reminded that "weeping may endure for the night, but joy will come in the morning!" (Psalms 30:5).

The Lord Knows, and We Do Too
(2 Timothy 2:19–21)

We have become so divided in our country today that it seems there is not a bridge long enough to cross the divide. What's so sad is that there are professing Christians on both sides, and it is sending out a confused message to unbelievers. How do we know a true profession from a false one? It may be from our standpoint at times hard to tell. But one thing is for sure. God knows, and he has given us a quality to look for in a professing believer to let us know for sure whether he or she belongs to him.

It seems on the surface that the foundation of our Christian faith is collapsing. But the good news is that Paul said it is sure. It is a foundation that can never be destroyed.

How does God know who are his? He looks into the heart. The Bible teaches us that he searches the heart. He knows the thoughts and intent of every person. He sees, hears, and knows everything about us that others do not know. He knows those who honor him with their lips but their heart is far from him.

How do we know who belongs to God? According to Paul, they who belong to God are those who depart from iniquity: "Let everyone that names the name of Christ depart from iniquity." It's pretty plain and simple. To be honest, any professing Christian that endorses a lifestyle or agenda that is contrary to God and the Bible cannot, in reality, be a follower of him. "They profess that they know God but in works deny him" (Titus 1:16).

So let us strive to be vessels of honor sanctified and meet for the master's use. "Sanctified" means set apart, and "meet" means useful.

Let there be no doubt whether or not we belong to Christ. Let us strive to be like Peter and John when they were brought to trial, and the religious leaders "took knowledge that they had been with Jesus" (Acts 4:13). There was no doubt about whose side they were on!

The Making of Something Beautiful
(Luke 7:36–50)

This is one of the most beautiful stories in the Bible. No wonder, Jesus said that wherever the gospel is preached, this woman's deed would be remembered. It is a beautiful story because at the beginning, it starts with an ugly life. The main character of the story is a woman who, on the outside, appears to be nothing but a wretched sinner but, on the inside, has the making of something beautiful.

Jesus has been invited to Simon the Pharisee's house for a meal. Simon, unlike the woman, is beautiful on the outside, but his inside would soon be revealed by his judgmental attitude toward Mary. He said, "If Jesus knew what kind of woman this was, he would not allow her to touch him." But Jesus knew her, and most importantly, he knew what she would become. How does this come about?

To begin with, Jesus looks at the heart. The attitude and motive of an individual is what he looks at when he makes an assessment of you and me. Jesus doesn't necessarily look at what we are as much as he looks at what we will become. In Mary's case, it was the beginning of something beautiful.

Then what he looks for is love. God, like you and me, wants to be loved. Of course, he wants to be respected, feared, worshipped, and adored.

But most of all, he wants us to love him. He desires that we love him with all our heart, soul, mind, and strength. Why? Because he first loved us. Even while we were enemies, he still sent his Son Jesus into the world to express that love through his death on the cross. The cross on the surface was ugly, but the work of it brought the beauty of salvation to all who believe. Psalms 149:4 says, "God beautifies the meek with salvation."

Jesus asked, "Which of the two loved much?" Simon answered, "The one whom much was forgiven." How much has God forgiven you? To what depth of love do you love him?

This is not the end of the story. It was this very woman who first saw the resurrected Christ. It was she that went and carried the good news of the resurrection to the disciples. This is the beauty of the gospel. The story of this woman's life had an ugly beginning, sitting on a dirty floor washing the feet of Jesus, but a beautiful ending in a fragrant garden proclaiming the resurrection. "Oh, how beautiful are the feet of them that carry the Gospel" (Isaiah 52:7).

It doesn't matter how much we have messed up our lives. Christ, through the new creation, can take that which is scarred, marred, or left for ruin and make something beautiful out of it. God said, "Behold I am making all things new!" (Revelation 21:5).

The Pain of the Cross
(Matthew 27:1–50)

One of the biggest struggles that many people have in accepting Christianity is the problem of evil, suffering, and pain. They say that if God is good, then why does he allow evil? Or if he is all-powerful, then why doesn't he abolish it? These are pretty pertinent and fair questions. My intention in this devotion is not to get into the cause of it as much as I want to address the reality of it in the gospel message.

First of all, God did not deny the reality of evil, suffering, and pain, but indeed entered into the reality of it through the incarnation of Jesus Christ. We need to remember that he didn't have to but desired to in order to reconcile the world of mankind unto God.

Second, not only did he enter into the world, he entered into the pain and suffering, feeling every aspect of it on our level and, in many ways, to a greater depth than we could ever imagine.

Finally, when we see his death on the cross, we not only see God suffering for us but with us. He suffered three types on pain on the cross, not only confronting pain but triumphing over it.

The first type of pain is *physical*. When we look at the physical pain that Jesus endured from his scourging to the beatings, the crown of thorns, the weight of the cross, and finally the nails, we see Jesus experienced a level of pain that most of us will never have to endure but deserve!

The second type is *emotional*. Christ, being the Creator of mankind, was rejected by his creation whom he loved, and this caused him much emotional anguish and grief. I had an old college friend who killed his parents a few years ago. I would have never thought that he would be capable of doing such an evil act. But that's the power of evil. The one thing I keep imagining, as an outside observer of this event, is possibly the look in his parents' eyes toward him as they lay there dying. I imagine this is the way Christ felt as he looked upon his creation that would become his murderers that day.

John said, "He [Jesus] came unto his own and his own received him not." I had an uncle who served two tours in Vietnam. The mental and emotional scars that he carried around with him for all his life, at times, were pretty overwhelming. In his time there, he witnessed and experienced things that he could not talk about, dealing with not only his own pain but, as a medic, the pains of others. But he told me that the worst pains were the emotions he felt when he came back home and was rejected, ridiculed, spit upon, and just simply ignored by the Liberal protesters of the day. I am sure that Jesus experienced this same emotional pain as he was rejected by his own people.

Finally, there is the *spiritual* pain. The Bible records seven sayings of Jesus on the cross. The one that describes the spiritual pain of Jesus is "My God, my God, why have you forsaken me?" Jesus experienced the greatest pain of all when God the Father had forsaken him as he became our sin-bearing sacrifice. No doubt, this is the hell of hell. To be separated from a loving God is the greatest anguish that one can experience. To enter in death without God is just the beginning of eternal evil, suffering, and pain. But thank God that this is the one pain that a believer in Christ will never have to suffer. He was forsaken so that we will never be forsaken in life or death.

In surveying these three types of pain, we see that God not only acknowledged the reality of evil, pain, and suffering but he conquered it through his death on the cross. Everything we experience in this fallen world, Jesus experienced and overcame it that we may have joy in sadness, patience in grief, a mediator in our struggles, hope in despair, and a peace in the midst of chaos.

Jeremiah asked a question in Jeremiah 8:22: "Is there no balm in Gilead; is there no physician there?" Yes, there is a physician, there is a remedy, and there is a cure all found in one person—the person of Jesus Christ!

The Pen and the Sword
(2 Peter 1:19–21)

"The pen is mightier than the sword!" This was a quote by English author, Edward Bulwer-Lytton. The point that he was making is that diplomacy is much more effective than violence. For most people, this statement is hard to believe. Most, if given the option when it comes to defending themselves, would logically pick the sword. But as I have grown older and wiser and in view of contemporary culture, I would have to agree wholeheartedly with Bulwer-Lytton's statement.

America, the greatest nation in the history of mankind, is on the verge of collapse. It has survived its world wars, cold war, and its war on terrorism. But the empire that is bringing down our civilization today is not one that has nuclear weapons, assault rifles, or tanks. This empire bears only one weapon—the pen! America's greatest threat and enemy has been the modern media.

Whether it has been through newspapers, social media, editorials, or music and literature, these outlets have had the greatest influence among the younger generation. Rhetoric has made its return, and because of the speed at which things travel on social media, once a statement is made—fact or fiction—it's out there and is left up to the subjective interpretation of the individual.

But we, as Christians, have the same form of weapon. In fact, what we have is greater than any media platform. We have the best of both worlds. We have the pen and the sword. We have the Bible!

The Bible was written by forty different men from various backgrounds. But its inspiration came from the Holy Spirit. It contains the gospel by which Paul said would be proclaimed by the foolishness of preaching. The written word being proclaimed throughout the ages has brought down the mightiest kingdoms and the toughest of men whose hearts were made a water as they heard the gospel. The writer of Hebrews says that the Word of God is "alive and powerful, sharper than any two-edged sword." It was the weapon that Jesus used to triumph over the lies of Satan in the wilderness, and it is the same weapon that has caused the church to endure throughout its history.

Andrei Sakharov designed the Soviet Union's RDS-37 nuclear bomb. He understood the power that this weapon contained to cause death and destruction. But after seeing the effects of it and the manipulation of world governments, he said, "I've always thought that the most powerful weapon in the world was the bomb and that's why I gave it to my people, but I've come to the conclusion that the most powerful weapon in the world is not the bomb, but it's the truth."

Jesus said that "heaven and earth shall pass away, but my words shall not pass away." What makes the Bible the most powerful weapon is that it is the truth. Modern news outlets and personalities may use their temporary power to promote lies and sway elections, but they will one day stand before a holy God and will have to give an account for the deception they spread through their Liberal propaganda. And by the way, the book that will be opened on that day by which God will judge all the human race will be the Bible. "Forever, oh Lord, thy word is settled in heaven" (Psalm 119:89).

The Bible is the written Word of God that cuts to the heart and brings men and women to the knowledge of the truth, found only in the person of Jesus Christ. Now that's good news.

The Pleasure and Power of Praise
(Mark 1:40–45)

In his book, *Reflections on the Psalms*, C. S. Lewis said, "I think that we delight to praise what we enjoy because the praise not merely expresses, but completes the enjoyment; it is its appointed consummation." In other words, when something brings so much joy to you, it is hard to contain it because the greatest part of the enjoyment is sharing the experience with others—things like a marriage engagement, a good book or movie, winning a ball game, killing that big buck, or catching the big bass. When something great has been done, the height of the experience is telling someone about it.

This is the way the leper felt after Jesus touched him and delivered him from his deadly disease. I can imagine that what he felt was "joy unspeakable and full of glory" (1 Peter 1:8). Jesus said, "See that you say nothing to any man: but go your way and show yourself to the priest, and offer for your cleansing those things which Moses commanded, for a testimony unto them" (verse 44). But as this healed leper now turns to leave, he couldn't help but to "publish it much and blaze abroad the matter" (verse 45). What had been done within this man had to be shouted abroad because that was the height of the enjoyment, being able to express to others what the Lord had done.

To praise God is one of the most intimate and meaningful experiences that you and I could ever enjoy. To tell someone what God has done for you personally is not only a praise but also a proclamation, a testimony to God's great love and kindness to mankind. To try to contain that within only leaves one unfulfilled because to share the experience only makes it more real, more satisfying, and, most of all, causes the Holy Spirit to rejoice within us.

In the beginning of Jesus's ministry, he touched and healed many, instructing them to tell no one. But after his death and resurrection, he commanded his disciples to "go and preach the Gospel to every creature." The leper proclaimed when he was told not to; we fail to proclaim when Jesus has told us to do so. That's why many

Christians today have never fully experienced the pleasure and power of praise.

I want to challenge you today to share your testimony or share something that God has done for you. People today need to hear that God is doing great things. The pleasure that you receive from doing it will bring glory and honor to God and will cause you to share in one of the most fulfilling experiences that can be enjoyed on earth.

The Triumph of Faith
(Exodus 1:8, Daniel 11:32, and 1 John 5:4)

For many years, the people of God lived in Egypt with peace and prosperity. Because of Joseph, they had found favor with the ruler of this mighty empire, and because of God's presence among his people, the Egyptians also shared in the blessings. But there was a Pharaoh who rose up who did not know Joseph.

Obviously, this new Pharaoh did not have any knowledge of Egyptian history or did not like how Egypt acknowledged Israel's God. All of a sudden, instead of seeing Israel as a blessing, he saw them as a threat!

It's amazing that an event that occurred almost 3,500 years ago is so familiar to us today. We too have been a nation that had been blessed by God and experienced the idea of biblical freedom as close as any other nation in history. We have had our blind spots and bad moments, but overall, everyone that has ever come to this country experienced the blessing and prosperity that can only be provided by our Judeo-Christian values. But now leaders have risen up who do not know God.

For the next few years, Israel in Egypt suffered under the rigorous ideas of this new Pharaoh. But the more the suffering, the more God's people prayed, crying out to God for a deliverer. It seems that this was a very weak moment in Israel's history, but actually, it was one of their best. We see in them the triumph of faith!

Daniel experienced a very similar situation in Babylon. Once again, God's people had been enslaved, this time for their sins. As they were exiled in a strange land, we once again see them at their best, crying out to God in prayer with hope, patience, and focus as they waited for those seventy years to be fulfilled. Once again, we see in their weakest moment the triumph of faith.

Daniel said, "The people who know their God shall stand firm and take action" (Daniel 11:32). Notice he said "they who know their God." Here is the great contrast and the encouragement for you and me today. We have leaders today in government who don't know Jesus, but we do! It may appear that this will be our weakest and most trying time in our lifetime. But they who know Jesus will stand firm and take the necessary action to be as faithful to him as they can possibly be. Who knows, maybe God—like he did with Moses—will send Jesus to gather his church together unto himself or, maybe like he did in Israel's exile, raise up a generation like Daniel, along with his three friends, to lead America back to God again. Regardless, we have a guaranteed victory.

John said, "This is the victory that overcomes the world, even our faith" (1 John 5:4). We will triumph because faith triumphs!

The Unspeakable Gift
(Luke 2:7 and 2 Corinthians 9:15)

I can remember growing up and getting that one gift each year that stood out above and beyond all the rest. It was something that I truly wanted, and words couldn't describe the joy and appreciation I had in receiving it. But the one gift I received that is the most appreciated came when I was an adult. It is the gift that keeps on giving and one that has brought much joy, peace, and contentment. That is the gift of God that I received in the person of Jesus Christ.

"Thanks be unto God for his unspeakable gift." The gift of his Son is one that is so full of love because God is love. He gave us himself! It is at such a depth of love that no one word or phrase can give it the credit it's due. Even one of the most emphatic, picturesque languages, the Greek language of which the New Testament was written, couldn't find a word weighty enough. John, the most thoughtful and spiritual of the gospel writers, used the immeasurable word "so." "God so loved the world that he gave his only begotten son" (John 3:16). So Paul doesn't even try to describe it, other than saying it is unspeakable. Although it can't be described, it surely can be felt and certainly can be seen.

How many of us have heard those stories about acts of kindness that touched our hearts and made us feel overwhelmed with awe? I have read the biographies of men and women who dedicated their lives to serving God and helping others in need. They take the gift of God's salvation and share it with others in ways that can only be seen because words will not do it justice. It is hard to describe the love of God that they have in their hearts and want others to have as well.

Many times, the gift of salvation has not been passed on with words as much as it has with hands.

Jesus came to earth to be that gift. He is the gift and giver. He grew up poor, and once his ministry began, he spent the last years of his life homeless. He was the lowliest of all men, yet what he gave is greater riches than what any man could ever give. Today he gives men and women not only what they want but what they really need, which are:

- forgiveness,
- victory over death,
- faith,
- hope,
- love,
- joy, and
- peace.

When Mary, the mother of Jesus, took him and wrapped him in swaddling clothes, I wonder if she really knew that while she was doing it, she was wrapping the greatest gift that the world could ever receive. That's why the gospel message is to receive the Lord Jesus Christ and you shall be saved. It is the word spoken that leads to a gift that is so unspeakable, and yet it also leads to a new life that speaks volumes.

The Wages of Sin and the Gift of God
(Romans 6:23)

"It is necessary that society should look at these things, because it is itself which creates them."

This is a quote from Victor Hugo's *Les Misérables* (book 2, chapter 7: "The Interior of Despair"). Hugo was inspired to write the novel about life in a failed, post-French Revolution era. He blames these conditions on society in trying to justify some of the actions committed by its characters. I do not doubt that there are some truths in what he says, but ultimately in order to cure the faults of society, we need to look at what society is made up of. It's made up of men and women, fallen men and women.

The problem with men and women is that they are "sinners." We do not like that word today because it comes across as judgmental. It is not a "politically correct" term. We water down certain sins, such as adultery, murder, theft, and lying, calling it free love, pro-choice, reparations, and subjectiveness. But looking at the outworking of all this, it is creating divorce and destruction of the family unit, bloodshed, looting, and a distrust in the media. All this produces death to a society.

Malcolm Muggeridge said, "The depravity of man is at once the most empirically verifiable reality, but at the same time, the most intellectually resisted fact."

What Muggeridge was saying is that when we turn on the news every day, we understand we have a problem, but nobody wants to call it what is really is—sin! Over the last sixty years or so, theology, psychology, and sociology have tried to deal with the fruit of our failed culture and policies instead of the root. The root of the matter is that we have turned away from God and, therefore, turned on one another.

When we turn away from God, it is we who lose, not him. We lose life, liberty, and happiness. We lose family, friendships, and the things we hold valuable, all in the name of not trying to offend someone or come across as dogmatic or judgmental. Thank God he wasn't worried about our feelings. He was worried about our souls. That's why he brought judgment upon his Son Jesus Christ on the cross.

Was this an offense? Yes! The Bible tells us so. But to them who are tired and weary of their sins and the wages of it on themselves and others, it is no longer an offense but a gift. The wage of sin is death. We can't deny it, for we see it every day. So let's call it what it is so that we may appreciate the gift of God in Jesus Christ more and seek to give it away. It is the gift that is everlasting, and it keeps on giving!

The Way and Weight of the Cross
(Matthew 16:24)

All of us have been in a store and have heard the crying and scream-ing of a child who doesn't get what he or she wants. It seems to be one of the first signs of the fallen nature in a child. The child thinks that a temper tantrum is a means to changing the mind of the parent to get what he or she wants. Some parents give in, only feeding and nourishing that selfishness that ends up hurting the life of the child instead of helping it. It hurts to go without the things we want, but over a period of time, we realize that those things we desired were either not good for us or not necessary.

Today we, as Christians, are feeling that we are not getting our way. We feel that what we wanted was what God wanted. And when it doesn't work out, we tend to be hurt, disappointed, let down, and, yes, even angry. Let's not beat ourselves up too much because what we desired was the best for our country, our churches, and, most of all, the generations to come. We meant well! But also, it is a humble reminder that God's ways and thoughts are much higher than ours (Isaiah 55:8–9).

This is when the reality of the gospel demands weigh in the most. It is then we learn the true meaning of Jesus's words here in our scripture: "If any man will come after me, let him *deny himself* and take up his cross and follow me" (emphasis added). By this state-ment, we learn that the Christian life is not about us but all about Jesus. That's why we too have to carry a cross. It symbolizes the death to self. Through the cross, we learn that life is all about going God's way and not our way. God's way is the way that leads to life, freedom, and that place where our life and history find its final fulfillment and triumph, when God's plan is complete and Christ reigns over all in eternity.

But not only do we have to surrender to the *way*, we also have to be willing to bear the *weight*. In times like these, we feel the weight and roughness of the cross. When times are good, the cross doesn't seem to be as weighty and rugged. But if you and I follow Christ long enough, we will experience the pain and suffering of dying to ourselves and accepting the will of God.

I remember many years ago when I worked with the United States Forest Service, there was an endurance test that we had to do once a year to prove that we were fit enough to fight wildfires. We would have to put on a backpack full of weights and climb up and down a short stairway. It was called the step test. We would have to climb up and down for several minutes. To begin with, it wasn't bad. But as time went on, the backpack got heavier, and the legs got weaker. We had to prove that we were fit enough to do the job.

Today you and I have something to prove. This is the true test of finding out if we are truly willing to deny ourselves and follow God. Are we fit enough spiritually to endure the weight of the cross that lies ahead? There may be many ups and downs ahead of us. I found in doing the step test that the going down was easy; it was the going up that was hard. Right now, God is leading us up, and we may be a little weary. But I am also reminded of the words of Jesus: "Come unto me all who are laboring and heavy laden and I will give you rest" (Matthew 11:28).

The way of the cross leads home, and the weight of it may be hard to bear. But as the hymn "The Old Rugged Cross" says, if we cling to it, we will "exchange it someday for a crown."

The Wonder of God's Love
(Ephesians 3:16–19 and Luke 2:8–18)

The last verse of the Christmas hymn "Joy to the World" mentions the "wonders of his love." This Christmas Day, we celebrate the birth of Christ two thousand years later and are still overwhelmed by joy and wonder at God's great love for us. The beautiful voices of that angelic choir lit up the night sky that illuminated the shepherds, and it was that light that carried them into the light of day when they first cast their eyes on the baby Jesus, who would become the light of the world.

I can imagine the overwhelming presence of God and his love in such a small child. No doubt, Jesus's birth was like any other ordinary birth, but the ordinary would give way to the extraordinary love that was wrapped up in swaddling clothes and placed in a manger. The shepherds, being the lowliest and most common of all men, were the first to witness such love and feel the love of God as it radiated from the Christ child. Not many were made aware that day of who this child was and what he would become, but as we reflect on it today, we know that those humble beginnings went on to change not only history but also many hearts down through the ages.

The lesson for us today is this. Just as Jesus grew, so did God's love. It was his love for mankind that led him to the cross, and when we survey the cross, we know that those four dimensions reached out in all four directions. And we are living testimony to the far-reaching power of the gospel and of God's love.

As we ponder on those dimensions that Paul wrote of in Ephesians 3:18–19, we are overwhelmed by the breadth, length, depth, and height of the love of God. It is unfathomable! I believe this is what inspired Charles Wesley to incorporate this "wonder of his love" into the hymn. If we ever lose that wonder, then we will have lost the most important aspect of the gospel message. That message is John 3:16: "For God so loved the world that he gave his only begotten Son that whosoever believes upon him should not perish, but have everlasting life." It is a love that is amazing, one to be admired and to be absorbed by the believer as the depth of God's love reaches the depths of our souls.

Just like those shepherds who guided their flocks in the wilderness that night, may we, as we wander through the wilderness of this world, wonder at God's great love and enjoy the fullness of his gift given to us in Jesus Christ!

True Discipleship
(Matthew 8:19–22)

I think that one of the biggest challenges for Christians today in times like these is not believing in Jesus but following him. Life consists of three things:

- duties,
- demands, and
- desires.

All three of these do present challenges in daily living and tend to get our focus off the real purpose in living, which is "acknowledging him [Christ] in all of our ways and he will direct our paths" (Proverbs 3:6).

Solomon, in Proverbs, used the word "acknowledge," and Jesus used the word "follow" in the gospels. Both words have the same meaning.

"To follow" means two things: cleave" and "conform."

When we follow Jesus as his disciples, we are to forsake all other things that hinder us and cleave unto him. In other words, we take hold of him and walk near him, allowing nothing to come between us and himself. This is what the disciples did when they left their boats, their nets, their collection seats, and even their families to go with him to preach the good news of the kingdom.

But not only does it mean to cleave, it also means to conform. "To conform" means to embrace his example in living and, if necessary, in dying. Jesus demonstrates to us what it means to be human and to live for God. He shows us what a proper relationship should be like between himself and others. He conveys to us the type of attitude that we are to have toward God and the world.

You see, when we understand the true nature of the disciple, then our *duties, demands, and desires* should not compete with our daily Christian living but enhance it, enjoying these things in his presence.

So are you just a believer, or are you follower of Jesus? There is a big difference between the two. Take a survey of your life at the end of the day, and the answer will be obvious.

True Worship
(John 4:4–29)

Worship is not a moment. It is every moment. This is the biggest misunderstanding in Christianity today. We have limited worship to just hymn singing or praise music at a certain time and place. It's not a new problem. It goes all the way back to when Jesus went to Samaria and met a woman at a well.

The Jews and Samaritans hated each other. Their hatred goes all the way back to when Israel was divided during the reign of Rehoboam. Jeroboam took ten of the twelve tribes with him and went north and set up places of worship in Dan and Bethel. They were divided over issues, such as race, equality, and religion. In the midst of all this conflict and confusion comes Jesus.

After offering her a drink of water from the wellspring on high and dealing with her sin, she wants to get into a religious scuffle about which is the right place to worship. The Jews believed it was the temple in Jerusalem. The Samaritans believed it was at Mount Gerizim. Jesus brings a solution to the problem by saying that true worship is not at a place but it is a person. "God is a Spirit, and they that worship him must worship him in Spirit and truth."

What this means is that worship incorporates the whole of life and not just one aspect of it. When we realize worship is not just limited to a church building but also to our workplace, in a deer stand, on the golf course, at Walmart, in a restaurant, then we see what Paul meant that "in every thing we do, whether we eat or drink, we do as doing unto the Lord."

There is not one isolated place or moment in which we set aside to worship. We strive to glorify God in every moment, every place, and at all times.

I love how this story ends. She said, "Come and see a man who knows everything about me. Is not this the Christ?" Notice she didn't say, "Come and see a place." No! She said, "Come and see a man." The invitation that the gospel proclaims is not to a place but to the person of Jesus. Our Christian witness is worship, and worship is witness. When we worship in the moment, at every moment, then the message will be that much more effective.

Trust Me
(Proverbs 3:5–7)

We all have had someone to say to us, "Trust me." With some people, we get an uneasy feeling when we hear that. Sometimes we put our trust and confidence in others, only to find out that those others really didn't feel certain about themselves. We do this because there are some things that are out of our control or our ability, and we have no choice. We are in one of those years where we see ads, interviews, or debates, and the person running for a political office looks you in the eye or into the screen and says, "Trust me." That leaves a lot of us really feeling uneasy.

"Trust me!" This is what God is saying to us every day. Our Scripture text tells us that there is one of two ways we can begin the day and go throughout the day.

We can lean to our own understanding or trust in the Lord.

Leaning on our own understanding is natural and sometimes okay if we have a good and proper understanding. But remember when you lean onto something, it must be solid and sturdy, or you are going to fall. Just mere human intellect alone will not guide us through life properly because we are more than just brain. We are heart. We are spiritual. We are limited in our vision, and some of the decisions we make today can adversely affect us tomorrow.

This is why having a personal relationship with God through Jesus Christ is important. Trusting in him is the first step we should take in our walk-through everyday life. We make that one-time commitment to him in faith as we confess our sins and repent, accepting him as a savior. But still, every morning, we must be determined and decide if we are going to follow him today or lean on our own understanding. Some people choose with their feelings, others with their lust giving into temptation, eventually falling into sin. This is why so many people today are lost. They have wandered away from the fold, and without the voice of Christ, our good shepherd and his Word, they grope around in the darkness of their unwise decisions. The good news is he will come looking for you, and when he does, one of the first things you will hear him say is "Trust me!"

God is asking us in everyday step, every decision, every moment of every day to depend on him and live life his way. Because Solomon would say two times in Proverbs, "There is a way that seems right unto a man, but the ends thereof are the ways of death" (Proverbs 14:12 and 16:25). Making the right choice is a matter of life or death. Choose life! Choose Christ!

In times like these, we need a voice and a vision that is certain. Christ and the Bible are that constant in an ever-changing world.

Meditate on these scriptures and the words of this hymn: "Trust and obey, for there is no other way to be happy in Jesus, but to trust and obey."

Two Pillars in Turbulent Times
(2 Chronicles 3:17 and 1 Peter 5:10)

In our Scripture, we have the description of Solomon's temple. I watched a visual tour of it on YouTube, and I was amazed at the detail and beauty of it. I can only imagine what it looked like in reality. There are many furnishings that stick out to us as we are guided through it, such as the Altar of Burnt Offering, the Brazen Sea, the Curtains, the Lampstands, the Table of Shewbread, and the Altar of Incense. As you move into the most holy place, there is the ark of the covenant and the cherubim. All these are amazing and point to the glory of God in the person of his Son Jesus Christ.

But two things that resonated with me in my current reading of this passage stood out the most. There were the two pillars. These pillars were called Jachin and Boaz. These two names have a symbolic meaning to the temple of Solomon and to us, the temple of the Holy Spirit.

First of all, pillars are used to hold up a structure. It was not uncommon to experience earthquakes in Israel, so whenever a structure was built, it had to be strong and enduring. Without it, the building could collapse and be destroyed. This presents to us an encouraging spiritual application today.

As God is shaking the earth and we are experiencing turbulent times, we, as God's people, are held up by the same two pillars and what their names stand for.

The first pillar Jachin means "God will establish." *Webster* defines "establish" as to "institute permanently by an act or agreement." We, as God's people, can rest assured that through the cross of Jesus Christ and the covenant made unto us through him, nothing we are experiencing can separate us from his love.

The second pillar Boaz means "God will strengthen." In these difficult times, it takes a lot of courage, patience, and focus to remain a source of strength to those in our churches and community. God has given us the task of remaining faithful to him. And in our times of weakness, by his sufficient grace, his strength will be made perfect in weakness.

I close with this verse from 1 Peter 5:10: "But the God of all grace, who hath called you unto his eternal glory by Christ Jesus, after that you have suffered for a while, make you perfect, establish, strengthen, settle you."

God has established us in Christ, and his grace is our strength. By these two pillars are we held up in our walk with God in times like these!

Under God
(Psalms 9:17)

Recently, there has been a lot of talk among Progressive Liberals about taking the words "under God" out of the Pledge of Allegiance. My question is this: If we are not under God, then who or what are we under?

It has been proven biblically and historically that man cannot govern himself. We learn that quickly in the first eleven chapters of Genesis. It was God's will for man to be able to govern himself by a conscience that was tended toward God and his laws. But Adam, in chapter 3, chose to be a law unto himself. Look at the results beginning in Genesis chapter 4 all the way down to our present day.

Read Romans chapter 1, and you see what happens to a culture that does not submit itself to God and live "under" his laws and grace. Modern political philosophy says that man can evolve without God. But Romans show us not evolution but devolution!

So who are we under then? Government? Look at how our cities who are controlled by atheistic Progressive Liberals are doing. They are under siege, under lockdown, under fire, under protest, under Marxist mobs, and underground for protection and safety.

And this is what America as a whole will be under if we fail to acknowledge and be under God.

This is why we, as Christians, need to continue lifting up Christ and the gospel, dwelling underneath the cross, abiding under the shadow of the Almighty. For when a nation forgets God, hell and evil has its day, and day then becomes night! For where there is no light, there is darkness!

Read Psalms 91 and meditate on the benefits of being under God.

Unspeakable Joy
(1 Peter 1:8)

The Christmas season has always been my favorite time of year. I start celebrating early, generally beginning around November 1, listening to Christmas carols and hymns, watching Christmas movies, and, of course, reading A Christmas Carol by Charles Dickens. But over the last few years since my daughter has moved away, Christmastime is an even more joyous occasion because I know she is going to be home for several days, and we get to make up for lost time in between visits. It is an inexpressible joy that you can't explain; you just feel it.

This is the type of joy Peter is writing about. He says that it is "joy unspeakable and full of glory." In other words, it is a joy beyond words and so indescribable that he can only refer to it as "glorious." What fascinates me is that he is describing a love for one in whom he says that his readers cannot see. Peter saw him, walked with him, ate with him, laughed with him, and cried with him. He was there when Jesus worked miracles, when he taught the secrets of the kingdom, and after his resurrection. There was no doubt that he shared many joyous occasions with Jesus in those thirty-three years.

Peter had the best of both worlds. He not only walked with Christ but, as the Bible teaches, Christ at this time of writing was walking in him. This was even more joyous because he knew that wherever he went and whatever he went through, Christ was with him. There were times when Jesus was in the flesh, and he would send Peter and the disciples to do certain tasks at which he stayed behind. But to experience the joy of Christ within him was far beyond anything Peter could describe.

The depth of love that Peter and we ourselves who know Christ have is one that unites us in a way that is much deeper than we could ever imagine. It is a love that produces a joy that resides in the depth of our soul and one that can only be there by the presence of him who brought joy to the world. It is not something that it seen, but it is felt, and nothing can separate us from that love because it abides within us and goes with us even to the far reaches of the world.

How can we love someone we can't see? It is simple! Just as I love my daughter in whom I don't get to see every day like I used to, I know that she is alive, doing well, and is accomplishing God's purpose in her life. I know that there is a coming a day when she will come home this Christmas season, and I will meet her at the door and give her a big hug. What a joyous time!

I also know that though I can't see Christ, he is alive and serving out God the Father's purpose in the world and in my life, and there is a coming time when he too will come to us and take us to his home and our home he has prepared for us. What a joyous time that will be, even more joyous because then we will see him! "Oh, what manner of love the father has bestowed upon us that we should be called the children of God!" (1 John 3:1).

Unto Them That Look for Him
(Hebrews 9:27–28)

One of my pet peeves is not being ready or showing up on time. I had a friend that was always running late and never took the time to call and let me know he was running behind. I believe in being ready and ready on time so that when the ride comes along or I'm picking someone up, there will be no delay.

This week, our Advent theme is on being prepared. Our Scripture ties together two of the greatest events in history, the incarnation and the second coming of Jesus Christ. Right now, we live in between these two great events but find ourselves closer to the later than the former. The incarnation consists of not only the birth of Christ but also encompasses his life, death, and resurrection. Verse 27 says, "It's appointed unto to man once to die; then the judgement." The writer of Hebrews has in mind the death of Jesus and the judgment he took upon himself for our sins so that we might be saved. Then he moves in verse 28 to the return of Christ and the expectation of "those who look for him."

So there are two things that we need to make sure that we are prepared for in this Advent season: death and the return of Jesus.

I want to ask you a question: When are you going to die? It is not one we like to think about, but nevertheless, it is one that must be confronted. We don't know unless we have some terminal disease and know that our time is limited. But even then, we can't put a date or time on it.

Another question I would like to ask is, when is Jesus coming again? Our Lord said that "no man knows the day or hour, not even the son of man" (Matthew 24:36). There have been date setters throughout the history of the church, especially in the latter times, that have tried to date it and were wrong. It is one of those great mysteries that we ponder and patiently wait to unfold in history.

The point I want to make is that we need to be prepared for both of them. We do not know when either will come, but what we can be assured of is that we can be prepared for either so that when it comes, it will not take us unaware. Being prepared means that we have made our peace with God through the death of Jesus Christ and looking for his coming again by living a life of holiness and looking for it today.

Jesus said in Matthew 24:44, "Be ready, for that day will come in a time you think not!"

Read also Luke 21:34–36 for further instructions on being prepared.

Voices
(John 10:1–11)

Jesus tells us that he can be heard. Imagine God speaking to you personally!

This is the privilege and joy of being one of Christ's little lambs. "My sheep," said Jesus, "hear my voice and another they will not follow." This is a peculiar trait among sheep. They are naturally inclined to draw near to the familiar voice of their shepherd and, at the same time, quick to withdraw from the voice of a stranger. What a lesson we have from our Lord concerning this unique relationship.

First of all, Jesus compares himself to one of the most looked-down-upon trades in Middle Eastern culture. Shepherds were considered the lowliest and most despised of all the working class in Israel. Yet they were the most necessary because of the need of lambs and rams for sacrifices that ensured the forgiveness of God's people. This identification with the shepherds was special in that Jesus is illustrating his purpose in coming as a meek and lowly savior to seek and save them who are lost. Not only does he identify as a shepherd but also the Lamb of God which would take away the sin of the world (John 1:29).

Second, Jesus imitates that love and care that God has for mankind. A lamb was the shepherd's most-valued commodity. Not only was it his livelihood but also, from a spiritual standpoint, he realized the importance of how every little lamb was to the people of Israel. Their whole relationship with God hinged on how well the shepherds took care and guarded their sheep. They were so valuable that, at times, someone would try to break in and steal them away. The shepherd would literally put his life on the line to save one little lamb. This also describes the heart of our Lord. Jesus came to take back everything that the devil (the thief) has stolen, killed, and destroyed in the human race. Jesus laid down his life for the whole world, but also, we can say he died for you and me!

Lastly, it teaches us that the relationship between shepherd and sheep is personal. The sheep hear the voice of their shepherd, and they will not hear another. There are many voices that are mentioned in the Bible:

- in the beginning, God said… (Genesis 1:3),
- the still small voice that spoke to Elijah (1 Kings 19:12),
- the voice of the Lord in Psalms 29,
- the voice behind you saying, "This is the way, walk you therein" (Isaiah 30:21),
- the voice of one crying in the wilderness (Isaiah 40:3), and
- the voice that was the sound of many waters (Revelation 14:2).

But the voice we strive to hear is the one that the Hebrew writer wrote of: "Long ago at many times and in many ways, God spoke to our fathers by the prophets, but in these last days, he has spoken unto us through his Son, whom he appointed the heir of all things, through whom he also created the world" (Hebrews 1:1–2 ESV).

God speaks to us today through the words of Jesus and his apostles who wrote the New Testament. Along with the voice of the Holy Spirit, he has communicated unto us the mind and will of God for the purpose of creation and history. But not only is his mind or will intended for humanity as a whole, God wants to communicate his mind and will to you and me personally. He wants to speak to us and communicate his love to us while he prepares us to be living sacrifices, holy and acceptable unto him, which is our reasonable service.

In a world that is full of voices today, where there seems to be so much uncertainty and lack of direction, seek to hear the voice of Christ in your life every day. I am sure that if you and I are sincere, we will hear a voice in front of us (not behind because Christ our shepherd leads, not we his sheep) saying, "This is the way. Walk in it!"

Wake Up and Get Ready
(Matthew 25:1–13)

There are so many applications that we can make from the parable of the wise and foolish virgins. It is a parable that has such great depth to it that a sermon could be preached on each verse, yet the message is so plain that one simple devotion can make one accountable to its truths.

The meaning of the parable is to *wake up and get ready*! During this season of Advent, that is the recurring message. There is such an eerie silence right now, and it leads many to believe that something big is about to happen. It could be the return of Christ or some major paradigm shift in history. Only God really knows, but regardless of what it is, God wants us to wake up and get ready for the upward call or outward call.

What I mean by "wake up" is this. I believe that with all that has been going on in the world over the last nine months with the pandemic, election, civil unrest, and hurricanes, all these have been an alarm clock for God's people. Never have we seen such catastrophe, confusion, and chaos like we are seeing now. Just as when the alarm goes off and wakes us from a deep sleep, we may feel a little stunned and confused before we gather our senses together and get up.

The meaning of the parable is that even the wisest and most devout of God's people have the tendency to become drowsy and fall asleep. The difference is that when the alarm is sounded, how are we going to react?

Will we wake up, light our lamps, and have enough oil? These are the things the wise virgins did.

170

What about the foolish virgins? They were slow to rise, slow to light their lamps, and prepared not enough oil to last until the bridegroom came.

Even though we do not know the day and hour of the Lord's coming again, I do believe that God will awaken his church one more time before it happens. This could be that time! Let us not hit the snooze button and drift off back to sleep. Let's get up, get ready, get right, and get going with our lamps shining that we, like a well-lit runway at an airport, can usher in the glorious appearing of our Lord and Savior Jesus Christ!

We Are God's Children
(Romans 8:13–14 and 31–39)

Martin Buber, in his *Tales of the Hasidim*, tells of a question that was brought to Rabbi Shelomo: "What is the worst thing that evil can achieve?" His answer was "To make us forget that we are each the child of a king."

Paul reminds us that we are children of God. One of the things that we encourage our children to do is to not bring embarrassment or reproach upon the family. We all want to be known as the parent of a child who has achieved some great accomplishment and not one that has committed a crime.

I think that's why it is important for us to remind ourselves daily that God is our father, we are his children, and we must remember that we should strive to honor, obey, and trust him. This is the whole premise of praying the Lord's Prayer on a daily basis.

When Buber says, "The worse thing an evil urge can do is cause us to forget that we are the child of the king," he is reminding us of the power of the flesh and how we can sometimes allow it to grieve and override the Spirit that is within us. Evil is always wanting to bring us down and can sometimes blind us to the reality that God has given us power over that evil and we dominate it; it does not dominate us. In times like these, when there is so much that is grieving and making God's people angry, the tendency is to return railing with railing or accusation with accusation. The temptation to get even or to "one up" someone is an urge that comes from pride that dwells deep within us, waiting to be manifested in challenging times. Paul reminds the believers at Rome that they are God's children and that God will fight for and defend his own.

We quote verses 31–39 in good times when it is easy to believe. But now, when things get difficult, we forget the strength and power that lies behind the words of Paul. We belong to God, and when the enemy comes against us, we need to remember that God is for us and that we are more than conquerors through Christ.

So what encouragement we have in knowing that our rightful place is in a kingdom where God is our father and Christ our king. Nothing will be able to separate us from him, but how you and I react to the evil urges that come from temptation and confrontation with others will either bring glory to his name or shame and reproach upon him. It's important in times like these to remember who we are, to whom we belong, and that our purpose is to glorify our Father in heaven.

We Need God
(John 15:1–11)

We need God!

It's hard to believe that this point has to be made so emphatically now in our day. But there is a growing atheism in America. And it has made its way into the political, judicial, intellectual, and social life of our country.

Jesus told his disciples that "they could do nothing apart from him." To live without him is to only end up in ruin. To die without him is to die lost and suffer eternity in hell. To govern a country without him is to turn it into hell (9:17).

G. K. Chesterton said that "there is a tendency to turn away from God, but if you do in heaven's name, what will you turn to?" Fyodor Dostoevsky said that "without God all things are permissible." When we try to live or govern ourselves without God, then it creates a vacuum for any or all things to be sucked in and take his place.

We see the outworking of this atheism today in the streets of Seattle, Portland, Chicago, and New York, just to name a few. This is why you see the lust for pleasure or power in people's lives today. That's why position, greed, sex, alcoholism, and drug addiction are at an all-time high. This is also why suicide is becoming a more viable option for many because without God, there is no purpose, meaning, fulfillment, or hope. Without God, Charles Darwin's nihilism becomes not just a theory but a reality.

With God, we not only have life but we have it more abundantly. By abiding in Christ, we will not only be fruitful but we "can do all things through him who strengthens us."

I personally learned a valuable lesson over the years. I used to think that my relationship with God was week to week. Then I realized that it was to be daily. Now what I have learned is that I need him every hour!

Focus on these passages of Scripture and think of the hymn "I Need Thee Every Hour" and see if you can't sense his presence today.

What Do You Think of Christ?
(Matthew 22:41–42)

What do you think of Jesus? I think that this is the most important question anyone can ponder, and it is most important that we have the right opinion of him. This was the question that Jesus asked the religious people of his day.

"Whose son is he? They said the son of David." This answer was partly right but, from a salvation standpoint, completely wrong. This was a half-truth, and half-truths are not the truth.

We live in a culture now where the person of Christ is judged by the Christians. This is putting the cart before the horse. Christians should be judged by the person of Christ, so when we do this, how do we stack up? Gandhi said that he "loved Christ, but did not like Christians because they were not like Christ." This is a legitimate argument on his part and one big hurdle that must be overcome, especially in our skeptical culture today.

The challenge for us then is to be as faithful to Jesus as we can possibly be and copy his example to the best of our ability through the person of the Holy Spirit. But, first, we have to get our minds right. How or what we think of Jesus will determine how we order our lives before a watching world. There is one place in which we begin. Before we can answer what we think of Jesus, we have to first think about Jesus.

Do you think about Jesus? Is he the center of your thought life? Are the decisions that you are confronted with every day made according to what he has revealed unto us in his teachings? Is the way you react and respond to situations in life determined by how he reacted and responded? How we think will greatly influence the outworking of our beliefs and the credibility that we give toward Christians.

Second, how we think of Jesus is determined by how well we know him. Is your knowledge of Jesus a personal one, or is it through secondhand knowledge? Does everything you know about Christ come from the preacher, or do you read and study your Bible and pray for the understanding of it? The better we understand the Bible, the better we understand God. C. S. Lewis said, "The Bible is to lead us to the true word of God, which is Jesus."

To tie all this together, when Christ is personal to us, then Christianity is not just a religion; it is a relationship. And if you and I are in a relationship with the person of Jesus, just as a husband thinks about a wife or wife a husband or parent a child, then we will think of him. If we are thinking of him, then we will think rightly of him.

Right thinking leads to right living!

Read and meditate on Romans 12:1–2.

What If
(Romans 10:13)

What if
I never surrendered,
Fully trusted,
And followed Christ?
Would I
Be content,
Feel meaningful,
Accomplished?

What if
I never saw
My need,
My sin, giving way to my pride?
Would I
Be empty,
Dependent,
Of a good conscience?

What if
I just went
Doing my own thing
At everyone else's expense?
Would I
Be lonely,
Be full,
Be loved?

What if
I were to suddenly
Grow weak
And flirt with death?
Would I
Be fearful,
Isolated,
And have no one to care for me?

What if,
In my despair,
Christ came walking
To my bedside?
Would I
Then listen
To his voice,
His word, his plea?

What if
I gave my heart,
My mind,
My soul to him in love?
Would he
Receive it,
Accept it,
As if it were his own?

What if
I acknowledged,
Confessed,
And turned to him?
Would he
Receive me,
Hear me,
And turn to me?

He would!

The Excellent Way of Love
(1 Corinthians 12:1–13:3)

It is said that actions speak louder than words. This is a biblically correct statement. Paul is writing about the manifestations of the Holy Spirit. They are referred to as the *gifts of the Spirit*. Some of these gifts are subtle in their manifestation, such as faith, wisdom, and discernment. But the majority of them are explosive in their manifestation, such as healings, miracles, and tongues with the interpretation of tongues. Having made known these gifts and before giving a description of how they are to be operated within the church, he talks about the most excellent of gifts or what he refers to as "a more excellent way."

That more excellent way is love. He says in the beginning of the thirteenth chapter that even though one possesses these gifts, if he or she doesn't have love, then it really all amounts to nothing. Love is the foundation of all great things done for God. The outworking of these gifts is most effective when built on the foundation of not only what God gives but what God truly is. He is love!

This most excellent way for many was a new concept in biblical times. Religion had become so abrasive and judgmental. Love had become lust, and the meaning of love lost was in the grossness of sexual perversion. Philosophy had spiraled down into meaningless and leaving one begging the question "Is there any meaning in life?" Without love, life is meaningless.

But in the midst of this cultural crises, God sent his Son into the world to redeem it. Why? Because "God so loved the world that he gave his only begotten Son." Through Jesus's life, death, and resurrection, we learn that love is more than just an expression of words; it is expressed through sacrifice. God's way is the most excellent way because it is the only way. God did not express the excellency and fullness of his love through prose, poetry, or roses. He expressed it in his Son.

You and I possess this excellence. It is not in our nature, but it is within us through Jesus Christ who abides within us. We surely have a treasure in an earthen vessel as Paul said, and this treasure is the greatest and most excellent expression of love. Let us, in this Advent season, ask God to manifest through us the greatest of all gifts, the gift of God's love wrapped up in our flesh through the Spirit of Jesus Christ our Lord who dwells within us.

The Father's Pleasure to Give
(Luke 12:32)

There are many misconceptions about God in our world today and for various reasons. One reason may be that people have not taken the time to research or investigate the evidence about him. Maybe they have had a bad experience with a church, or it could be that some Christians have misrepresented God. Of all the misconceptions, the one that I think is the most misconceived is that "God wants to withhold or hold back mankind." According to the Scripture in our text, that is far from the truth.

Jesus said it is "the Father's good pleasure to give you the kingdom." This is not withholding; this is opportunity! In the realm of God's kingdom, there is unlimited freedom and liberty. Christ has set us free from that which has held us down and back, which is the power and dominion of sin. Paul mentions in Roman 6:17 that we were once the servants of sin. We yielded ourselves to the works and ways of the devil, but through Christ and the work of the cross, we have now been made free from sin and become servants of righteousness (Romans 6:22).

So now we have the freedom to do and to be the man or woman that God had created us for in Christ. We live under grace and the gospel, not under the law with all its restraints. Does this mean now we have a license to sin? In the words of Paul, "God forbid!" No, it is not a license to sin but a potential to do righteousness and to have peace and joy in the realm of the Holy Spirit (Romans 14:17).

In this Scripture setting, Jesus is giving his disciples another portion of what he shared with them when he gave them the Sermon on the Mount. In that sermon, he is not talking about doing; he is talking about being. He is talking about becoming. No, there is no holding back or holding down. It's about becoming the person that you and I have always longed to be, a person like Jesus! One of the first lies the devil told to Eve was "God is holding you back because he doesn't want you to be like him." God does want us to be like him. He wants to conform us to the image of his Son. That's why he did not hold back his best from us when he sent Jesus to die for us.

In Romans 8:32, Paul said, "He that spared not His own Son, but delivered Him up for us all, how shall He not with Him freely give us all things?" We do have a God that does want to take. He wants to take us unto himself and give us himself. He is unlimited in his person. And being and when he is in us and we are in him, there is unlimited power, joy, peace, and, most of all, opportunity!

What Is God Like?
(John 14:1–9)

I am currently reading a book of which I will leave the title and author unnamed. In his chapter titled "God," he basically said that the world would be better off without him. The basis of his argument is that in our pluralistic culture, there are so many religions, with so many interpretations of who God is, how he acts, what he expects, and what happens when we humans don't meet those expectations. One strength in his argument that I can't deny is that there have been atrocities committed in the name of God, such as the Crusades, the inquisitions, and the conquering of nations and bringing about oppression all in the name of advancing the kingdom. As an honest lover of history, the accusations are true. And it is embarrassing to see how greedy, covetous, and power-hungry churchmen have used God's name in vain.

But that does not mean we don't need God? We desperately need him. But in the midst of all the confusion, which religion is right? And how do we know for sure? In order for God to be God, there will always be a certain mystery about him. Without it, we lose our wonder of him. Yet there is also a necessity of being able to identify and know him because what he desires the most is a relationship with each individual human. Only Jehovah, God of the Bible, has unveiled himself enough to show us who he is and what he desires. This unveiling came not just on parchments, paper, or prophets; it came in a person.

Jesus, in our Scripture, just revealed to his disciples that he was going away to prepare a place for them. Thomas said, "Lord, show us the way." Jesus said, "I am the way, the truth, and the life. No man comes unto the Father but by me." Thomas wanted to know the way, but Philip wanted to see the Father. What Philip was asking is what any child or even an adult may ask at one time or another. What is God like? Do we look at history for the answer? Do we look at a church for the answer? Do we ask some religious leader? No, we look to Jesus!

Jesus responded to Philip by saying, "If you have seen me, you have seen the Father." Jesus is "the fullness of the Godhead bodily, the visible image of the invisible God." That is why it's important that we read the gospel regularly and study the life of Jesus. In doing so, we will see the personality of God. We will see how he acts, thinks, and deals with mankind. Jesus not only shows us what God is like but he also shows us what man should be like as well. He is our example.

So yes, we need God, but not just any god. We need the God and Father of our Lord Jesus Christ who is the way, the truth, and the life and leads us into an intimate relationship with him that we may know him personally.

I would encourage you to write down any questions about God that you have and pick a gospel to read. See if Jesus answers those questions for you.

When Are We Going Back Out?
(Mark 16:15–16)

In talking with many pastors and laypeople over the last few months, I hear this question on a regular basis: "When are we going to be able to go back inside the church?" It is obviously a reasonable question, and I understand the nature of the urgency. We miss the comforts of our sanctuary, our Sunday school classes, our choirs, and, most of all, the hugs and handshakes. To some people, it just isn't church if we don't get back to the way that we were. So I understand the question, but there is another question that I would like for you to think about. That question is "When are we going to be able to go out of the church and share the gospel?"

Jesus said to go into all the world. The only world that we have been going to for many decades now is "our little world." We have been going to church week after week, and that's about the extent of many people's Christian life. We are happy going in and hearing the gospel in song, prayer, or preaching but never have the burden of doing those things in the workplace, family get-togethers, mission work, or places of recreation.

I personally feel discouraged sometimes because all I do is preach to churchgoers. We are living in a time where the gospel should be good news. Yet we are not seeing conversions; baptisms are down, and there is no concern about becoming disciples of Jesus. Most people are just content about being saved and going to heaven.

The gospel is more about earth than heaven. It's more about living than dying. It is about surrendering our lives to Jesus and becoming followers of him through faith and repentance. It is about conforming to his image and allowing him to live out his life in ours.

So I am not as much concerned about when we are going back in as I am about when are we going to go back out and fulfill the Great Commission. Jesus said go, and we must obey!

Where Are You Laying Your Head?
(Judges 16:1–20 and John 13:23)

How bad it was for Sampson to wake up and think that he could just put on his strength after toying with Delilah. This was the fourth time he mocked her, but unfortunately now he is the one who is being mocked. He did not know that the Holy Spirit had left him. Ultimately, Sampson's problem was not in toying with Delilah; he had been toying with God!

We may play games, but God doesn't play games. We are at a point of crises in our country today, and God's people are like the children in the marketplace crying out. "We played you a wedding song and you did not dance and we played you a funeral song and you did not mourn" (Matthew 11:16–17).

Sampson used his strength and power for his own selfish desires, never really taking his calling seriously. He never did as Peter encouraged to "make his calling and election sure" (2 Peter 1:10). Sampson had forgotten that he had been purged from his sins and needed this terrible reminder that his strength had come from God and the Nazarite vows that he promised to keep.

The application for us today as God's people is that we think that we are going to wake up after the election this year and everything is going to be okay. We think that everything is just going to work itself out as always, not really taking seriously the threat of losing everything that this country has stood for and has been blessed with. If we are not careful, we will wake up like Sampson thinking that we still have God's blessing and favor, only to realize that we have lost our freedom of religion, our freedom of conscience, and, most of all, our laws that give us the right to life, liberty, and the pursuit of happiness.

Unless we elect to put God first, it doesn't matter who we elect for political office. This election is not about who is running as much as what platform they are running on. One has God in its plans; the other doesn't. We need to use the strength of our wisdom for good, not use it like Sampson for one's own selfish gain. We need to practice loyalty to our God and not family tradition to one party or the other. We need to choose our bed appropriately before we lie down on the night of the election, or we will wake up not knowing that the Spirit of the Lord has left us! The challenge for us is to stop laying our heads in the lap of the Delilah of indifference, worldliness, and unbelief and do as John did on the night before Jesus's death on the cross—to lay our heads upon his chest and hear the heartbeat of his love and compassion for us that we may be united unto him in love and faithfulness.

Remember Peter said, "Judgement begins at the house of God" (1 Peter 4:17). He that has an ear to hear, let him hear what the Spirit is saying to the church!

Where Does God Work?
(Philippians 2:12–13)

God works!

Most people have this idea that God is sitting up in heaven just observing all that is going on. Some do see him at work in the universe holding everything together. Others see him working in and through national leaders as he raises them up and brings them back down again, fulfilling his providential purposes. Most Christians see him at work in his church carrying out the Great Commission and advancing the kingdom of Christ.

All the above are true, but the one way we fail to acknowledge God is his working within the believer. Paul points out that most of God's work is done in and through the Christian, working to accomplish his providential work in their lives. He also makes the point that this work is not just something that remains inward but has an outworking to it accompanied with fear and trembling.

Jesus was and still is a carpenter. He framed the world by his Word. He built a bridge, by way of the cross, to fill the gap between God and man dug out by sin. And even now, he is at work in the lives of the saints, bringing forth the fruits of righteousness which are the pillars of his kingdom.

Paul said in Ephesians 2:8–10 that we are saved by grace through faith and not of works. Salvation is not our work but his work alone.

Yet through faith and by his grace, he is still building you and me up as a habitation for his Spirit. Verse 10 says, "For we are his workmanship created in Christ Jesus for good works." He not only created us to be good but to do good, and that good work is done by him, in and through us for his glory.

In times like these, it is when we are seeing the outworking of evil by Satan and his demonic forces producing hate, violence, corruption and division through the media, politics, and hate groups that we, as God's people, allow the Holy Spirit to work in us producing good works and hope for a world in despair.

God takes pleasure in this work, and when we present ourselves as clay that is willing to be shaped and molded, it is then that we have the pleasure and satisfaction that comes through serving him.

Where Is God?
(Psalms 10:1)

As I write this, there is yet another hurricane that is threatening to make a landfall into the Gulf States. This will be the fourth one this season, and there is still a ways to go. The devastation of wind, floods, and storm surge has done billions of dollars in damage, not counting the physical, emotional, and spiritual damage done to the residents. This is just one aspect of the chaos in this present year. There are wildfires out West, civil unrest in our major cities, and, to top it all off, a pandemic. I also need to mention that it is an election year.

David, in our text, feels that in the midst of evil and destruction, God is just standing aside as an onlooker or casual observer. Sometime he feels that God is not even there and that he has left the world to run its course and play out its destructive themes.

When we sit back and try to take it all in, it can be pretty overwhelming. We used to wake up to our normal routines, but now we don't know what to expect when we wake up. What will—or shall we say what can—happen now? When I contemplate the issues at hand, it is then that I began to meditate on the Word of God. It says when we meditate upon it, we shall be like a tree planted by the rivers of water. In other words, we will not be tossed to and fro or be rooted up by the winds of chaos around us.

I think about the time God spoke to Job in the whirlwind. Job's life and theology was rather chaotic and fleeting, yet in the midst of it all, God was not only speaking but present in the storm. God said to Job, "Where were you when I laid the foundation of the earth?" The Lord immediately let Job know that he was the Creator of all things and was in control.

I also think about Moses meeting God at the burning bush. Moses, living a much different life after fleeing Egypt, has now met God, who is not only speaking from the fiery bush but also present in it. As Moses saw his kinspeople suffer, he heard God saying, "Let my people go!"

I also think about the civil unrest that was taking place in Jerusalem, but at the same time, I hear God speaking through the prophet Jeremiah of better days that are to come when he says, "I know the thoughts I have for you, thoughts of good, not of evil, to give you an expected end."

Even in a plague, I can still hear the voice of God as he passes through Egypt on the night when the firstborn was taken, saying, "Stay indoors" and "When I see the blood, I will pass over you."

We may feel like those disciples on the stormy sea being tossed to and fro, fearing for their lives. Yet on board, there is Christ who rises up and says, "Peace, be still."

Even as they see him after the resurrection and he ascends up to the throne of God, we have his promise: "Lo, I am with you always, even unto the ends of the earth."

You see, when we move from contemplating events to meditation on the Word, we will find out that not only is God speaking to us, he is also present with us, right here in our own storm in times like these.

Where Is the Promise?
(2 Peter 3:1–12)

Advent is a time of expectation. In it, there is a longing for redemption, reconciliation, and restoration. Israel longed for the coming of the Messiah. We too have been waiting a long time for the second coming of Christ. Every new Advent season, I imagine that this could be the last one before Christ comes. Many Advents have gone by, and still, there was no return. Yet there will come one Advent season that will be the last, and to the redeemed that ushers it in, it will only be the beginning of an eternity with God.

There were some in Peter's time that grew weary of the promise. They were skeptically asking, "Where is the promise of his coming?" Peter assured his readers that just as God flooded the earth in Noah's day, he would "melt the heavens with fervent heat" at Christ's second coming to judge the world. Peter is trying to encourage watchfulness and the engaging in prayer by hastening the day of Christ. In other words, what will usher in his return will not necessarily be some great event but a church crying out, "Even so, come Lord Jesus!" (Revelation 22:20).

Until then, we see the patience of the saints and the patience of God being manifested in the world. The patience of the saints is seen in its enduring suffering and focus on sharing the gospel. The patience of God is seen in the fact the he doesn't want anyone to perish but give all the opportunity to repent. So the challenge before us in this Advent season is patience in waiting, focus on reaching the lost, and praying, "Even so, come Lord Jesus!"

God keeps his promises! Paul said, "The promises of God are in him [Jesus] yes and amen!" (2 Corinthians 1:20). Let these three challenges be our guide as we celebrate this Advent season. And who knows, maybe this will be the year of our Lord!

Who Is on the Lord's Side?
(Exodus 32:1–26 and 1 Peter 1:2)

The doctrine of election is one of the most controversial doctrines in all of theology. It has been the fuel for an ongoing war between Calvinist and Armenian believers ever since the Reformation. Did God choose us, or did we choose him? Do we as humans even have a choice? These questions have been fought over for centuries and will probably continue to be until the Lord comes again.

My viewpoint is not from a dogmatic closed system of belief. I take it for what it is. Election means that God, you, and I have a choice. It is what makes God who he is, and it is what makes you and me different from the rest of creation in that we are made in God's image. Like God, we have the ability to make choices, to have emotions, to feel, to will, and to be creative.

So looking at this concerning God's electing, I rejoice in the fact that, after the fall, God chose to save Adam and Eve. He elected to not only keep them alive but also decided that they both, with the whole human race, would be redeemed through the death of Christ, the seed of the woman. God was not forced to do this, but of his own free will, he decided to do this against those who rebelled against him. This is the beauty of love! "Love," by definition, means choice.

Man's electing to choose God is the same. God does not intrude or force himself upon anyone. Man has a free will and can choose or resist the grace and salvation that is offered in Christ. What makes us decide this is that there comes a point in time when we are illuminated to the truth of the gospel. The foolishness of preaching and the Holy Spirit at work convicting of sin and convincing of righteousness and judgment to come brings one to the knowledge of the truth. So election, in one sense, means two parties are choosing the same thing. One according to mercy, the other according need, and both on the bases of love.

Having understood all this helps me to not only know how to choose in salvation but also how to choose in life. We are in an election year, and our political affiliations have made our nation become polarized to such an extent that there seems to be no help or hope for our country. But here is a simple solution.

Let us, as Christians, cast our vote to God! Let us be loyal to him and not to our political affiliations. After the giving of the law, the children of Israel broke all the commandments and made a golden calf to worship. The Scripture says that the children of Israel rose up to play. Playing politics is not a playing matter when our streets are full of bloodshed, violence, immorality, teenage pregnancy, poverty, sickness, broken families, and so forth. The golden calf we have made of our political circles will lead to our undoing. It's time to grind it up and turn back to God!

Moses said, "Who is on the Lord's side?" That is what I am asking all who reads this today. It really doesn't matter what your family history has been according to political affiliation and issues. Times have changed since Great-grandpa and Great-grandma have voted. But God doesn't change! Keeping in mind that he chose to do right by saving us and we chose to accept the way, the truth, and the life of Jesus Christ, let us align up with him and not do what's right for our party but do right for the kingdom of God!

Who Is This?

(Song of Solomon 8:5)

Who is this coming up out of the wilderness,
leaning on her beloved?
It is the bride of Solomon, one in whom he adores.
Why is she leaning?
His closeness she implores.

Who is this coming up out of the wilderness,
leaning on her beloved?
It is the bride of God, one he has redeemed.
Why is she leaning?
She is wearied from slavery in Egypt and of freedom long dreamed.

Who is this coming up out of the wilderness,
leaning on her beloved?
It is Judah, after seventy years reprieved.
Why is she leaning?
In Babylon, she grew weary, longing to leave.

Who is this coming up out of the wilderness,
leaning on her beloved?
It is Mary with child from above.
Why is she leaning?
She is laboring with child, the Son of God's love.

Who is this coming up out of the wilderness,
leaning on her beloved?
It is the bride in whom Christ would die.
Why is she leaning?
Because she was born through blood and water
out of his side.

Who is this coming up out of the wilderness,
leaning on her beloved?
It is the church, all battered and bruised.
Why is she leaning?
She was hated because of the husband that she
did choose.

Who is this coming up out of the wilderness,
leaning on her beloved?
It is the people of God, their way not comprehending.
Why are they leaning?
For they lean not to their own understanding.

Who is this coming up out of the wilderness,
leaning on her beloved?
It is the church who has been revived.
Why is she leaning?
She has not full strength to yet flourish and thrive.

Who is this coming up out of the wilderness,
leaning on her beloved?
It is the ageless woman of Christ's youth.
Why is she leaning?
She has grown tired through laboring for truth.

Who is this coming up out of the wilderness,
leaning on her beloved?
It is those who have overcome death.
Why is she leaning?

She has been brought back to life by his life-giving breath.

Who is this coming up out of the grave in the end?
It is the dead in Christ.
Why are they leaning?
Because upon his grace, they lived their lives.

Who is this coming up out of the wilderness, leaning on her beloved?
It is you and me, his own.
Why are we leaning?
Who else is there to lean on?

Why Am I Discouraged?
(Psalms 42)

There are many reasons as to why people suffer with discouragement, despair, and even depression. It is not only nonbelievers who suffer these things. Many believers do so as well, even those believers in the Bible. Moses, Elijah, Jeremiah, and the writer of Psalms, David, all experienced one, if not all, of these in their service to the Lord and his people.

There are many contributing factors that lead people to feel this way. They may suffer the loss of a loved one, a job, investments, or a failed marriage or could have mental imbalances brought on by certain illnesses, disease, events, or medication. Sometimes, the loss of interest or mounting pressure can put one into a place of despair.

David was experiencing a time when his soul was "cast down… it was disquieted [chaotic] within him." It was not unusual for him to feel this way when you read about his life or read the Psalms that he wrote. He was hated and had his enemies from within his country and outside of it. He had his family issues and, oh, by the way, the reaping of some of his sins. But what was unusual about this particular time was that he didn't know why he was feeling the way he was. He said, "Why are you cast down, my soul?"

It is normal to experience this, but if we are going to experience this state of mind, we need to at least know why before we can ever get deliverance. Are there legitimate reasons for it? Sometimes when we think about it, the reason why we feel the way we do is simply because we worry about things that aren't there or things that we can't control. We can build up scenarios in our mind and create a supposed reality when, in reality, it is not real at all. These things are created by a spirit of fear, and if we are not careful, we can allow it to blind the mind of faith in God and cause us to feel separated and isolated from him.

So if you are experiencing this, ask yourself the question why. David said unto his own soul, "Why are you cast down?" Then respond the way that David did as he encouraged himself in the Lord by saying, "Hope in God." Finally, he would offer up a sacrifice of praise which would stir up the gift of God within him.

God is not as far away as the devil would have you to think. David refers to God as a stream in verse 1. Jesus told a downhearted, thirsty woman at Jacob's well that there is a well and a drink of water that would satisfy her ever longing. That well is one that springs up from within. It is a well that is deep. It runs from the "depth of God's love to the depth of our soul" (verse 7). That well is Jesus. He is with us always, even unto the end of the world. He is the health of our countenance (verse 11).

You Are Not Alone
(1 Kings 19:1–18)

Elijah had the unfortunate task of preaching the word of the Lord to Israel in one of its darkest periods in history. They had fallen under the sway of King Ahab and his wicked, idolatrous wife, Jezebel. After his victory on Mount Carmel in the previous chapter, he now finds himself running for his life as Jezebel has put a price on his head. As a result, this powerful, highly anointed man of God becomes weak and discouraged. He has become depressed and just simply wants to die.

The reason he wants to die is not that he has lost a savor for life but that he feels that he is all alone and the only one left who is loyal to God. In his lowest depth of mind, we see the height of pride rise up in his soul: "It is enough now, oh God. Just let me die... And I, even I only am left." In other words, what Elijah was saying is "There isn't anyone else saved but me." This sets Elijah up for an eye-opening revelation.

We too are experiencing a time of darkness in our country like never before. Since the nineties, we have seen such a decline spiritually and morally, and it's all due to our turning away from God. This follows the pattern of Israel seeing how we too had a great revival on the eighties in the evangelical circles of Christianity. Having lived during that time, it is very discouraging right now to see the collapse of our culture and the turning of our backs on God. The biggest temptation for us today is much like Elijah. We feel that we ourselves or our church or denomination are the only ones faithful to God in this backslidden age. We can be no further from the truth.

No matter how dark the times may get, God has and always will have a church and a remnant faithful to him. Some will be seen, and some will work behind the scenes. But nevertheless, the Lord knows them that are his. God spoke to Elijah and said that there were "seven thousand that had not bowed a knee unto Baal." God was telling him that there are many others out there that have not turned away from him, for the number 7,000 is a symbolic number meaning an untold amount. Elijah couldn't see them, but God could. And this was not only a rebuke to Elijah but also an encouragement.

So this is a reminder to us all. Though it appears that the majority of our country has turned back, there is a silent majority of God's people that are praying, witnessing, and living for him and in due time will be made known. The light of God's church will shine in the darkness, and the darkness will not be able to overtake it.

For further study, read John 1:1–5 and 8:12 and Matthew 5:14–17.

You Have Deceived Me
(Jeremiah 20:7–9)

I am sure that most, if not all of us, are feeling let down and disappointed this morning. The results of the election have seemingly not gone the way we thought or prayed that they would. We feel in some way like we have been deceived. We are not the first of God's people to experience this.

Jeremiah's indictment to God was "Thou has deceived me, and I was deceived." He felt like God had toyed with him, and now he is greatly hurt. He also has become a mockery to his enemies as they ridicule him for believing that God would act on his behalf. He had been faithful to bring forth God's Word to the people, and the more he did, the more they ridiculed him and imprisoned him. Not only did he feel he was about to lose his country, he was also about to lose heart.

Today we feel the same. We feel that we are about to lose our country. Everything we have gained back in the last four years may be lost again. We could be going into our own type of exile, and we have already had a taste of imprisonment with the COVID-19 and the lockdowns. The threats coming from the Progressives are now more of a reality than before, and faith could be the first item on their agenda.

Some may feel like never voting again or praying again and even trusting again. Jeremiah felt this way and was on the verge of never speaking in God's name again. But then another feeling arose in him. This feeling and emotion lay deeper than any other. It was the fire that he felt burn in his bones by the Word of God. "His word was like fire shut up in my bones…and I could not stay." No matter how hard he tried, he just couldn't give up.

One other illustration is the disappointment of the two disciples on the road to Emmaus. They had believed that Jesus was the one to redeem Israel, but they saw him die, and they lost hope. Yet even in their disappointment and despair, Jesus joined himself to them and, starting with Moses, told them about the things he would have to suffer. As he did this, the hearts of the disciples burned within them.

So don't lose heart! Are we disappointed? Yes! But we need to remember that although we feel let down, God is with us to lift us up. He has not and will not forsake us but will be with us where we need him the most—on the altar of our souls as a burning fire that cannot not be held down or held back!

You Sound Like a Christian
(Matthew 26:73 and Colossians 4:6)

I was in a coffee shop in Virginia several years ago. As I ordered a cup of coffee, the young lady behind the counter looked at me and said, "You are from North Carolina, aren't you?" I responded by asking, "How did you know?" She said, "Your speech gave you away."

Peter's speech had betrayed him. It sold him out. He could deny Christ all he wanted to, but his speech gave him away. In pressure moments, what is on the inside will come out.

I think it is important for us as Christians to be saying the right things in the moment. We are under a lot of pressure in our country right now, and it is on the verge of boiling over. People's personal opinions and affiliations are being made known, and the picking sides of good and evil are lining up. How do we know what side a person is taking? Listen to what they say and how they talk.

Peter was a Galilean. This was the most common identification mark among Jesus's disciples. So when he talked, it was obvious who he followed. What are you saying today? What are you talking about the most? Do you, in response to all the politics today, affirm the Bible? Is that the answer you give?

In listening and reading about what people are saying and writing, I am afraid that most people line up with Republicans or Democrats, Trump or Biden, Conservatives or Progressives. Politics and policies are all necessary issues that need to be discussed, but only in the light of what has been revealed in the Bible. Listen to yourself speak. Jesus said that whatever is in the heart comes out. If you support that which is ungodly and promotes death over life, darkness instead of light, then your speech has betrayed you. Would you say you are a supporter of Republicans, Democrats, or Jesus? If it is Jesus, then you will speak like him!

It is not only important to speak like him, we need to speak for him. We should seek to use the tone of which he used in communicating truth. Today, there is so much hatred and bitterness that even Christians, instead of pulling society up, have lowered themselves to their level. Paul said in Colossians 4:6, "Let your speech be always with grace, seasoned with salt." In other words, our speech should be favorably toward God and tasteful. Salt does three things. It preserves, seasons, and, most of all, creates thirst.

So let us show our identity during this day of division. Let us make it known whose side we are on. Let us speak those things that edify and build up.

About the Author

Robby Stewart is the pastor of Crestview Baptist Church in Rockingham, North Carolina. He is the author of a previous book, *For Such a Time as This*, of which *In Times Like These* is a follow-up book. He is married to Vickie, and they have two children—Kennedi, married to Jared Henry, and Jeremiah. Pastor Robby not only serves his church but also is a chaplain to various agencies within Richmond County and has served on various boards. His hobbies are reading, hunting, and playing golf.